Families Are Forever

...if I can just get through today!

Families Are Forever

... if I can just get through today!

Janice Madsen Weinheimer

Deseret Book Company
Salt Lake City, Utah
1980

First printing in paperbound edition, March 1990

Library of Congress Cataloging-in-Publication Data

Weinheimer, Janice Madsen, 1937–
Families are forever—if I can just get through today!

Includes index.
1. Weinheimer, Janice Madsen, 1937–
2. Mothers—United States—Biography. 3. Children
—Management. I. Title.
HQ770.W44A34 301.42′7 79-17807
ISBN 0-87579-320-7

Printed in the United States of America

10 9 8 7 6 5 4 3 2 1

Dedication

To Beckie, Debbie,
Russell Eric, Kerry, Kyle, Jackie,
Julie, Wendy, and Tanya
—the noble spirits entrusted
to our care

Contents

Acknowledgments

To all the many friends and acquaintances who over the years have suggested that I write a book, I am grateful. The idea grew from them. But the motivation came from the continual prodding of my daughter Beckie, who insisted that I put this story on paper.

Emmett R. Smith was my "coach" and spent hours counseling, reading manuscript, and advising me. To him I am deeply grateful.

To my son Kyle and my husband, Gerald, I am much indebted for their encouragement and hours spent in proofreading.

To Charlene and Steve Elcock I express heartfelt thanks for their constant push toward the goal line and their vote of confidence.

I especially appreciate the professional advice and efforts of Eleanor Knowles and Emily Watts of Deseret Book in the editing of the manuscript, and of Ralph Reynolds for the design.

I am most grateful to all my children, who provided me with the experiences that were the basis for this writing, and to my own dear mother, who taught me by example as well as by precept to love and serve the Lord first.

Chapter 1

Nearest to God's Love

"Number one's a girl," Dr. Brown said, as he placed the baby on my stomach and began tying off the cord. One minute later he said, "Number two's a girl." Five minutes later he placed the third baby on my stomach and said, "Number three's a girl."

Then the doctor turned to the nurses and urged them to get the premature babies cleaned and down to the incubators quickly. They had arrived two months early, and he was concerned about their survival.

The room had been congested with every available intern and nurse watching the multiple birth. Dr. Brown had asked my permission for observers to be present during delivery because multiple births weren't the usual occurrence, and this was an opportunity for the young doctors and nurses to learn. I was somewhat hesitant, but my husband told me I wouldn't really care who was in there once the delivery started (and he was right). So I gave my consent. It seems ironic, however, that everyone else could watch the delivery except my husband. Fathers weren't allowed in the delivery room in those days.

Suddenly the door to the delivery room burst open and in rushed a young doctor. He scanned the room quickly and asked, "Is it all over?" He heard several affirmative replies, but walked over and rubbed my stomach anyway, to make certain for himself. "I guess that's all," he said. If I had had a free leg, I would have kicked him; for a doctor, he displayed an appalling lack of empathy.

Now that the delivery was actually over, my mind became alert to the fact that I had once again had my prayers answered. When I knew I was having a multiple birth again (I had had two sets of twins previously), I had desperately wanted at least one girl. And the Lord had sent me three!

I remembered the first time I had wanted a girl so

desperately. My mother had asked me what I would do if the Lord chose to send me a boy. "He won't," I had replied flippantly, "or I'll send him back." That was my first pregnancy, and I was obviously very immature. But for some reason the Lord had been good to me and had given me a darling baby girl that first time.

Beckie was six now, the oldest of eight children. She had been a pure delight and as nearly perfect as a child could be. It was a blessing that she had been a girl—with so many small children, I depended on her help with the household chores when she was still very young.

I reflected on Beckie's birth and the feeling I had had then. As a teenager I had never been particularly interested in babies. When my brothers and sisters had brought their new babies home, all the rest of my family were excited and oohed and ahhed, while I was almost totally uninterested. Once my older sister came and stayed with us for a week after her baby was born. My younger sister bathed the baby and cared for her and couldn't understand my disinterest. I didn't even hold the baby while she was there.

The opportunities to babysit were very rare when I grew up, as we lived in a rural area. I tended babies only twice, and was almost totally unattached to them. I had considered myself lucky to have been born next to youngest in my family: that way I had only one little sister with whom I had to help. Tending her had been a real chore for me and not one that I enjoyed.

My mother and sister had come to visit me the afternoon after Beckie's birth. I was still under the effects of the anesthetic and was only vaguely aware of their conversation as they sat and discussed my little Rebecca. "Did you ever see so much black hair?" "Isn't she a beautiful baby?"

That night as the nurse placed Beckie in my arms, I turned to look at her. "This surely can't be my baby," I thought. "Why, she's not beautiful at all." She was all red-faced, and with the swelling across her nose and the mass of black hair she looked like an Eskimo baby. I was quite disappointed. "They've made a mistake and brought me someone else's baby," I consoled myself.

The next day, when I kept receiving the same baby, I became convinced that she was truly mine. Gradually the feelings of motherhood began to be born within me.

The first night home with any new baby is a memorable

experience, especially if it's your first child. I can remember my first night home with Beckie as vividly as if it were yesterday. I lay in the bed with the bassinet right next to me. I hardly dared to breathe, I was listening so intently for Beckie's every breath. I must have sat up and checked her fifty times that night to make sure she was still alive and breathing. She had suddenly become so precious to me that I begged Heavenly Father to protect her and keep her alive. I was so frightened of losing her that I couldn't sleep. A thousand thoughts crossed my mind that night—two of them I remember well.

I had never been particularly close to my own mother; I had been a somewhat rebellious child and had caused her a good deal of heartache. She really didn't understand me, and I didn't choose to help her either. But that night I began to gain an appreciation for my own mother. I had never really thought that she loved me, and so it came as quite a shock to me when the thought entered my mind that my mother had probably experienced these same feelings concerning me that I was now having for Beckie. I couldn't help shedding a few tears and thanking the Lord for the mother I had misunderstood for so long. Oh, how much I had to learn!

As the night wore on, my thoughts focused on a loving Heavenly Father who had chosen to let his son sacrifice his life in our behalf. I thought of the Savior, of his suffering in Gethsemane and at Golgotha hanging on the cross, and my heart ached as I began to realize for the first time how terribly hard it must have been for the Father—who has greater love than we can even imagine—to allow such an act to take place. Somewhere, too, wasn't there a heavenly mother whose soul was wracked with agony for her son? And what about Mary, as she stood so near and yet so helpless? My heart throbbed as I too cried for the Savior and for his mothers who painfully watched his suffering. I checked Beckie again and wondered why God was so good to me when I deserved so little.

Each time I brought home a new baby, I seemed to relive this first night. The constant checking for breathing and the fright of losing such a choice little spirit always chased away any chance for sleep. And again, each time I remembered my mother and the Savior and the sacrifices they had made for me.

Now, anticipating caring for three new babies, I reflected upon the words of President Joseph F. Smith: "The love of a true mother comes nearer being like the love of God than any other kind of love." (*Gospel Doctrine,* p. 315.) How grateful I was to be a mother again, for my soul was filled with such a love that perhaps only mothers can truly understand.

Chapter 2

Caring for New Babies

I watched intently as the nurse changed Beckie from hospital garb to the lovely baby clothes I had made for her. I didn't know much about babies, and I had suddenly become aware that her care would now be my responsibility. What a challenge for me!

Beckie was such a good-natured baby that she wasn't much of a problem to take care of. She slept through the night the first day we took her home, and continued to do so. Through the day she awakened automatically to be fed every four hours, as if she had a built-in timing device. So in this regard life was easy.

Bathing was another situation, though. I was scared to death to put the baby in the water. My sister-in-law came over and showed me how to do it. She had just recently had her third baby, and she was a natural. I watched intently as she folded the towel by the sink and laid Beckie on it. She filled the sink partway with water and felt it with the inside of her wrist to make sure the temperature was just right—not too hot and not too cold. Then she undressed Beckie, handling her gently and talking sweetly to her all the time. I took in every detail.

She dampened the washcloth in the water and carefully washed the baby's face and ears. I noticed how she kept part of the towel across Beckie's body. She told me new babies weren't used to being uncovered, so I should keep a towel over them. She kept a tight hold on both Beckie's hands with one of hers and explained that the position a baby is in before being born keeps his hands and legs tucked in toward his body. After he's born he has more freedom without control. This causes his legs and arms to flop around, and the flopping frightens him. When you're holding his hands together, they can't flop, and it makes the baby feel more secure.

I remember how she took hold of Beckie's right arm with her

left hand and rested her arm under Beckie's head. Then she carefully used her right hand to support Beckie's body, and lifted her gently and slid her easily into the water. She kept her at an angle so just her bottom and legs were in the water. She used her free hand to handle the soap and finish the bath.

When she had rinsed Beckie off, she carefully lifted her onto the towel and quickly covered her with it. She patted her gently with the towel rather than rubbing her. She was careful to put baby powder around her neck and under her arms and to rub it in gently. This was to help prevent chafing, she told me. I noticed she poured the powder onto her hand away from Beckie so the powder didn't get into her face. I asked her not to put powder in the baby's diaper area as the doctor had told me it could cause problems with female babies.

I watched that bathing so intently because I was so frightened to do it that even today the details remain vividly implanted in my mind. I soon learned, however, that bath time is a very pleasant experience with a baby.

Beckie was such an easy baby to care for that I began to wonder what was the matter with mothers who talked so much about the work involved with having babies. Of course, I had nothing to compare her with, and so I didn't really appreciate what a rare gem I had.

How soon all that was to change! The Lord had done a reversal in my case: he had given me the blessing first, and all the work came after.

Beckie was not quite two when a twin brother and sister arrived on the scene, five weeks premature. We knew we were having twins so it wasn't a shock—at least not the fact that there were two. Most other things were a shock, however.

The initial shock was when I left the hospital and was compelled to leave my babies there for a few days. I had learned a lot about being a mother in two years, and now a mother's love and concern were natural for me. My husband took me home and was planning to go back to work. I was so distraught having had to leave my babies, however, that he decided he'd better stay with me. Those were torturous days for me.

It was exciting to bring Debbie and Russell Eric home from the hospital, but frightening, too. Dr. Snow, our pediatrician, cautioned me about them. I hadn't had premature babies before. Eric seemed to be doing fine and was on a four-hour feeding schedule. Debbie was more frail and needed nourishment more often. She was on a three-hour schedule.

Having two babies on different schedules was certainly tiring. I was grateful I had decided to stick to schedule feeding with Beckie, because I didn't have time to worry about a system with Debbie and Eric. I doubt that I could have told when Eric was hungry, anyway, as he cried almost constantly.

After nursing two babies for a while, I was almost worn out. I hadn't had over two hours' sleep a night for three months. Debbie was quiet and had much the same nature as Beckie, though she had to be fed more often the first two months. But Eric was totally different. He cried so violently that a pacifier wouldn't even stay in his mouth. I remember walking the floor one night with him. Actually, it was five o'clock in the morning, and I hadn't even lain down yet. My husband just peacefully slept through it all. I sat on the edge of the bed with Eric screaming. Gerald didn't even stir. I started to get angry: I was so tired, so totally exhausted, and there he lay peacefully asleep. "They're his children too," I thought, beginning to cry. "It just isn't fair."

That day was Easter Sunday, and somehow I had managed to make Beckie a new dress in spite of my schedule. My brother and his wife came to visit in the afternoon and to see our new babies. They were the first twins in the family, and so they had created a little excitement.

My sister-in-law took Beckie on her lap and talked to her, commenting on her new dress. During their playful conversation she said, "Have you been neglected with all the attention this new brother and sister are getting?" That really pricked my conscience.

That night I made some new resolutions, and the next day I put them into practice. First of all, I decided to quit nursing. I had given the babies a good start, and they were doing well now. By feeding them with a bottle I could have more help; I'd have more time to spend with Beckie and I could be a better mother. I also taught Eric to suck his thumb. Drastic measure? Maybe, but it worked, and I wished I had done it long before. It pacified him and satisfied his sucking desire. He turned out to be a model baby after that.

I learned a great deal from those three months. One thing was that I would never nurse a baby in the middle of the night again. When we brought our second set of twins home two years later, I was better prepared. With them, the 2 A.M. feeding was done by bottle, so my husband could help. He soon learned to appreciate me more! He had never gotten up with a baby in the night before.

Have you ever watched a nursery full of new babies? Some are crying; some are sleeping. Have you ever thought about babies being able to sleep through noise?

When we brought Beckie home, we were storing a television set for a friend of mine. I placed the T.V. in the living room by the wall common with the bedroom, then put Beckie's bassinet next to that wall in the bedroom. I would turn the set on frequently while she was sleeping. I did this purposely to get her accustomed to sleeping through noise. It was otherwise very quiet in our home then, as she and I were there alone during the day.

I never tiptoed around. I never worried about the doorbell ringing. Noise simply didn't disturb Beckie because I didn't train her to sleep only when it was quiet.

Can you imagine the trauma of trying to keep five little children—ages six and under—quiet while triplet sisters are trying to sleep? I had trained my children to sleep through noise so well that when the triplets were sleeping I could go in and vacuum under their bassinets. I'd move them around, and it didn't disturb them. Beckie was the only one for whom I had had to provide the noise; there was always plenty around after that.

Once we went to visit a member of my husband's family. When we got to the door, there was a little sign saying: "Please don't ring the bell—baby asleep." I had seen signs like that before, but it still shocked me. We went in, and I had a terrible time trying to keep five little children quiet so the baby could sleep. The mother tiptoed around and everyone spoke in whispers. I respected her rights, and if she chose to live that way, that was her decision, but I couldn't exist like that. I told Gerald I couldn't go visiting there any more with our children.

Have you ever heard a mother say, "I could manage through the day all right if my baby would just sleep through the night?" I have learned from listening to many such mothers that they train their babies to wake up in the night. I chose to train mine to sleep through the night. I didn't learn this all at once. Beckie never awakened during the night, so I had no such experience with her. Debbie and Eric, being preemies, awakened regularly during the night at first. But Debbie was soon sleeping through, and after I taught Eric to suck his thumb he began to sleep through also.

When we brought Kerry and Kyle home, we used our new system of bottle-feeding in the night. After we had fed them, burped them, changed them, and made sure of their comfort, we put them back to bed. If they cried, I got up and checked once to make sure everything was all right. If they continued to cry, I went back to bed. I didn't always sleep, but at least I rested.

I arrived at a formula of my own for when a baby should sleep through the night. Kerry and Kyle had been born five weeks early, but they were bigger babies and adjusted more easily than Eric and Debbie had. I decided a baby should be able to sleep through the night by the time he is nine pounds or three months old, whichever comes sooner.

If my children weren't sleeping through on their own by then, I began to train them to do so. If they had reached nine pounds or three months and were still waking up, I let them cry it out. They might cry for half an hour or so the first night, but eventually they would fall back to sleep.They might even wake up in an hour or so and cry for a while again. I might have to feed them, but if I could stand it long enough to make them wait an extra hour or two, I had made a start. Sleeping longer soon became a habit, and they began to go for seven or eight hours. They'd usually wake up only one or two nights and then go the eight hours, or they might work up to that length of time gradually. They might sleep five hours and then cry incessantly and refuse to go longer, so I'd have to feed them. The next night they would perhaps go five and a half hours before I'd have to feed them. The next night they would go six hours, then seven hours, and finally eight hours.

This formula for sleeping through the night is based upon a 10 P.M. feeding. We didn't want them to give up the 10 P.M. feeding before the 2 A.M. one, so if they would normally sleep till 11 P.M. or so, we needed to wake them at 10 P.M. and feed them. We also needed to train them to have their awake time between 6 and 10 P.M. to make this plan work satisfactorily. We would hold the babies and keep them awake for several nights from 6 to 10 P.M. until staying awake then became a habit. Then they were more willing to go five, six, or even eight hours before being fed again. This may sound like a lot of work in the beginning, but it only takes a couple of weeks before the babies are well on their way to sleeping longer when we're used to sleeping.

Some babies seem to come with a built-in mixed-up schedule. They're awake all night and sleep all day. But habits like this can be reversed if we work at it and retrain them. It usually takes three weeks to form a new habit, so we shouldn't give up.

I have learned that generally our children learn to do what we train them to do. If we continually give them a drink every night, we are training them to wake up for it. If we rock them to sleep each night, we are training them not to go to sleep until they have been rocked. If we put them to bed with a bottle, we are teaching them not to go to sleep without one. I was very careful never to put a baby to bed with a bottle because I realized if I did, someday I would have to break the habit. I fed my children in another room, changed them, and then put them down for the night. They whimpered some, but they soon learned to fall asleep on their own.

When Beckie was still small, I put her down for the night at 6:30 P.M. She cried nearly every night off and on till 8 o'clock. I kept checking her and wondered what was wrong. After several nights, I got smart and put her to bed at 8 o'clock. She went right to sleep. After that I put her down at 8 o'clock and had no further problem.

When I used a pacifier with Beckie, my mother really didn't like it. She used to take it out and would say, "Let her cry. It will do her good. She'll have healthier lungs." When she'd leave, I'd give Beckie the pacifier again. One of the books I read said a new baby has an intense desire to suck that is satisfied between the ages of three to four months—if he is allowed to suck as much as he desires. I found this to be true. I gave each of the children a pacifier (which Eric couldn't keep in his mouth). I let them suck as much as they desired for the first three months. Between three and four months their desire waned, and I threw out the pacifiers. I had two thumb suckers: Eric, whom I taught, and one of the triplets. I never did anything to stifle this, as I'd studied just enough psychology to know not to frustrate them. I never worried about it, and they gave it up on their own after they were two years old.

I found that holding a baby a great deal the first three months didn't seem to spoil him. The spoiling seemed to occur after the age of three months. Then a baby got used to it and seemed to demand it.

One mother told me that neither of her children had ever slept through the night, and the oldest was four. I stared at her in disbelief. I couldn't imagine anyone who liked to get up in the night so well that she would continually get up every night and get her children a drink. I need my rest more than that. My children had to learn to live with me—not me with them.

Several women have tried my formula for training children to sleep through the night and have found that it works. Even mothers who have seven- or eight-month-old babies who have never slept through the night have applied the formula with success. It's not always easy. If you have older children, they may complain at the crying, but suggest they get up every night and take care of the baby, and they're quickly pacified.

Chapter 3

Establishing a Routine

A new baby in the home tends to disrupt a regular routine. The baby's needs are met first and everything else becomes secondary. This isn't a hard-and-fast rule, of course, as sometimes a baby has to cry while other crises are met. But usually the baby comes first.

Not being able to accomplish as much as I had before the baby arrived bothered me until I found out that if I allowed three to four months for the baby to get on an established schedule and to get away from night feedings, I could reorganize my routine so that I could accomplish as much as I had before. Sound impossible? Well, it's not, and it really works.

This is one more thing in favor of "scheduled feeding." You know pretty well when the baby will wake up and how much time will be required to meet his needs.

For instance, after three to four months, the baby has given up the 2 A.M. feeding. He may still be eating around 8 to 10 P.M. and again around 6 to 8 A.M. My desire was to get the baby to be able to go twelve hours at night without a major feeding. I usually fed him a bottle at 8 to 10 P.M. time; then in the morning when he awakened, I fed him orange juice and tried to get him to go till about 8 A.M. for more nourishment. This way I could feed him cereal at the same time I was giving the other children breakfast, and we could all be together. The older children enjoyed watching the baby while they were eating, and I could also take care of my husband and get him off to work between the orange juice and the cereal.

The next feeding would come when the other children were eating their lunch. I would have their lunch ready before the baby woke up, and would feed him vegetables and fruits while they were eating. I'd finish with a bottle for the baby while I was encouraging the other children to finish their lunch.

Dinner for the baby might have to be done around 4 P.M., but the other children were usually hungry by then too, and they appreciated a nutritious snack while baby was being fed. Then they were more content to entertain baby while I finished preparing the evening meal.

Essentially this program means that the baby was on three meals a day (with the other children) except that I was giving him juice earlier in the morning and an extra bottle of milk before bed at night.

As a baby grows and is able to handle finger foods—bananas, toast pieces, etc.—he may be pacified with this and be willing to wait till 5 P.M. for his dinner along with the other children (and husband too, if he arrives home that early).

By the time my children were seven months old, I tried to have them eating three meals a day—with us and right from the table. I made my own baby food with a blender, and when the children were around five and six months old I began to chop their foods less fine (like purchased junior foods). After they could handle the chopped foods well, I started feeding them with us. This meant I had to be a little more careful in planning my menus to include foods the babies could eat.

I also started giving the babies drinks of milk from a glass when they were four months old. True, it was messy at first, but they learned. By the time they were seven months old, they usually drank well enough from the glass that I could get rid of the bottle. I tried to make the switch before the baby became attached to the bottle, when it would become a problem to have to take it away from him. I tried to always outguess the baby and be one jump ahead of him. It saved lots of problems later on—crying on the baby's part and frayed nerves on my part.

With the arrival of the triplets, I had to work out a little different program to be able to accomplish as much as I had before. At the noon feeding, I put them all in their infant seats and lined them up on the counter or on the table. I then fed them in a line-up—a spoonful for each in turn. It took little more time to feed three this way than it had to feed one in my arms.

I could still coo and talk to them all the while I was feeding them, and they could see me easily. I learned that by using pillows I could feed a bottle to one baby by the side of each of my legs with the bottles propped, and hold the third in my arms. I rotated the one who got held each time so each one would feel mother's love and caress, but they could all still see and hear me.

For the cereal feeding I invented my own feeder, as commercial ones weren't available then. I heated an extra-large needle on the stove and put it through the nipple of a bottle to create a large hole. Sometimes I got the hole too big and ruined the nipple; I had to experiment to get it just the right size so the baby didn't get the cereal too fast or scream because it was too slow. It was much quicker to feed this way, but by hand feeding the fruit and vegetables at noon, the babies also got used to being spoon-fed. As they got older, I included their egg yolk in their cereal, which was a simple way of getting that down.

Organizing my time in feeding the babies this way allowed me to have time to accomplish the other things I needed and wanted to do.

One of the things I had neglected with my first children was my study of the gospel. I had established excellent habits for regular gospel study before my marriage, but somehow with all of my new involvements my study habits had become erratic.

Before I was married, I got up early and spent half an hour in gospel study and then some time in prayer and meditation. I really missed the special spirit that this seemed to create for each day. Now that I had a family, there didn't seem to be enough time to get the sleep I needed, let alone organize time for gospel study.

One day when I was nursing my first set of twins; my mother came for a visit. After I had finished and had the twins in bed, she told me how she had always studied the gospel while nursing her children. My mother had an excellent knowledge of the gospel and was considered an authority by many people. Still, it upset me when she told me this. I felt she was preaching to me as if she felt I was wasting time. But after I cooled down, I pondered for quite a while on her advice. After a night's sleep, I realized the value of what she had said. I began that very day to read while I nursed. By the time I had quit nursing when the first twins were three months old, I had completely reread the Book of Mormon and half of *Sermons and Missionary Services of Melvin Joseph Ballard.*

I had learned a great deal from that study. Almost more important than the gospel concepts I learned was the fact that the days when I read and studied the gospel and took time to have my private prayers were my better days. I had more patience and more love, and things in my household ran much more smoothly. I was also able to accomplish more. Seeing such good results from this new habit, I was determined that it would continue. I vowed I would at least read the Book of Mormon once each year. I have kept that vow faithfully and have read not only the Book of Mormon, but other good books as well. In recent years I have tried to make it through all the standard works. It usually takes me more than a year to finish all of them, but I still keep up with the Book of Mormon yearly.

This has made a great change in my life, and I highly recommend it for all mothers. By spending some time in gospel study and prayer each day, you will be able to accomplish more and have a better attitude. Martin Luther said something like this: "I've got so much to do today, I'll have to spend an extra hour on my knees to make sure I accomplish it." When we're doing what the Lord asks of us, we're more in tune and more able to accomplish our goals.

Having children also distorted my shape, and I learned early the value of exercise. The only regular time I could find at first was before going to bed. I was so tired by then that it was more of a chore than it should have been. I kept at it, however, particularly after being so stretched out of shape with multiple births. I remember particularly how discouraged I was after the triplets were born. I went down to shower in the hospital and the attending nurse took one look at me and said, "You don't look like you've even had your baby yet." That didn't do much for my morale.

But that wasn't the worst. When the doctor released me, he told me to go home and wear a girdle around the house for a while to help pull my stomach back into shape. I was willing to do anything, as my shape was obviously very noticeable, so I went home and proceeded to try to stuff my stomach into a girdle. It was like trying to stuff bread dough into a balloon, but I finally made it. I let go of the girdle, and it quickly rolled back down. Even the girdle couldn't hold me in. I was so discouraged that I sat down and cried. The next day things looked better, however, and I began my exercise program. It took six months of exercising half an hour a day to get my stomach back into any kind of respectable condition. I couldn't do that half hour of exercising all in one session; it was done one exercise at a time all during the day, whenever I could sneak a few seconds.

When exercise programs on television were in vogue, I was

usually able to work my schedule to fit them in. I ran to do other things during the commercials so as not to waste time. This was good for my children also, as they became exercise enthusiasts at a very early age.

When the Canadian government came out with its 5-BX program, my husband also became interested in exercise, so I joined him in his program. We usually did our exercises before retiring. I found out it wasn't so bad to exercise before going to bed if I had someone to do it with. This also gave us an extra bit of time together.

Whatever a mother's schedule is, exercise is important. It not only helps keep her in shape, but she feels better and is able to accomplish more. It's an important ingredient of health, which is vital for all mothers.

Chapter 4

All's Quiet at Church

When Beckie was approaching her first birthday, she began to be a handful at church. I was determined that my children would behave at church, but my knowledge and experience were very limited.

About this time, we went to visit my brothers in Idaho. Since we were there over the weekend, we attended church services with them. One brother had a boy just three weeks older than Beckie, and I couldn't help noticing how quiet and complacent his son was while Beckie was very active and quite a handful. I asked him how he managed to keep his son so quiet and content. He told me it doesn't just happen; you have to work at it.

I wasn't afraid of work, and I decided that if all it took was work, I'd tackle it. I began by sitting and holding Beckie on my lap at home for nearly an hour each day. She wasn't allowed to get down from my lap or have toys to play with. She had to learn to sit still. If she wouldn't, it was easy in the home atmosphere to talk to her about it and be firm with her while no one was watching. She was a very easy child to train, and she became so much in tune to reverence at church that as she got older she folded her arms when we got out of the car at church and wouldn't unfold them till the meeting was over. One of the counselors in the bishopric told me how impressed he was with her reverence. He told me how one day in Junior Sunday School one of the deacons bumped her with the sacrament tray and water spilled all over her shoulder and down her dress into her lap. She didn't move a muscle but kept her arms tightly folded. He said she didn't move even when he quietly went over and wiped her off.

Beckie was an exception. I soon learned that. The others weren't nearly as easy to train, but nevertheless, they were trained. We found out that taking books or toys or dry cereal or other foods to meetings was more of a problem than a help. Children who had nothing to play with or to eat were less fussy than those who had toys and food. Besides, I was taking my children to the Lord's house, and I wanted them to learn to respect it as such, not as some place to which we go to play and eat.

It wasn't easy, and sometimes it was quite frustrating, particularly when other people could see us struggling and would offer our children a toy or something to eat. Or else our children could see things other children had and would want them. But still I was determined.

Training two or three at a time to sit still for an hour each day takes quite a bit of time—at first. But it's worth all the time and effort in the long run. After working at several different methods, I finally arrived at a satisfactory training program for reverence.

When a baby reaches his first birthday, he's old enough to start training. This means that the mother will need to plan an hour each day when she can sit and hold him without interruptions. She should plan it during the other children's nap time, if possible. She should have a church book for her to read—preferably with no pictures. This way she can get caught up on her reading while she's sitting each day. I used to prepare my Mutual lessons during this time. The baby is to sit still on mother's lap during this time. He's not allowed to get down, but has to sit quietly. When he struggles to move, she simply says "No," firmly, and tightens her hold till he relaxes. He may whimper or cry a few times at first. She can talk to him kindly and tell him he has to sit on her lap. She should tell him she loves him, but he must learn to sit still so he can be reverent in Heavenly Father's house.

As with most new habits, it takes about three weeks for this one to form and become a part of a child's life. Some more difficult children may resist longer, but even they will eventually give in. Husbands need to help with this program so that the baby learns to behave for either parent. Both parents should be patient and ask the Lord's help. He will bless their efforts.

After the child has been trained, and during his training, if he misbehaves at church we should simply take him out, talk firmly to him, and go back into the meeting. This will reinforce the training he has been receiving at home. We shouldn't stay out, however, or we may be training the child to cry so that he can get out and do something else. We may have to leave the meeting several times at first, so we should sit on or near the back row. Above all, we shouldn't resort to crutches. The cereal, books, and toys should be left at home. Children should be taught when they're young that church is for quiet learning, not for playing and eating.

If we go out of a meeting with fussy children and don't return to the meeting, but rather let them run and play in the hall, what are we actually teaching them? Let's look at it closely:

1. We're teaching them that if they want to go play in the hall, all they have to do is whine and cry.
2. We're teaching them that they can get out of things they don't want to do by making a fuss.
3. We're teaching them that they can get their own way if they make a loud enough noise.
4. We're teaching them that what they want is more important than what we want.

Then when they're older, we wonder where they ever learned such actions, never realizing that we trained them right from infancy to act that way.

If they are fussy and we take them out of a meeting, talk to them, and bring them right back in, we are teaching them:

1. That what goes on in the meeting is important.
2. That they are expected to stay for the entire meeting.
3. That they are expected to act in a positive way during the meeting.
4. That we expect them to be obedient.

As our children got older, we allowed them to sit on the benches by themselves, but they were not allowed to climb up and down. They had to sit there. Of course, sometimes they had to be reminded, particularly after a new baby arrived and our attention was distracted from them. By the time the triplets arrived, our other five children could sit quietly during the meeting with only an occasional reminder.

Our children were taken to the bathroom before meetings and weren't allowed to run out for drinks and trips to the rest room during a meeting. Occasionally a situation arises where it is necessary for them to leave the meeting and return, but this is the exception and not the rule.

When our second twins were still quite young, I wanted to

sing in the choir. We were still working on our reverence program. My husband was willing to take the other four children if I would take one of the younger twins with me. The thought of having to take a misbehaving baby out from the choir seats on the stand was mortifying to me, but my desire to sing in the choir was so strong that I finally decided to risk it. I tried really hard to train my children well, and each Sunday as I prepared for sacrament meeting I told the Lord my situation. I told him how I wanted to sing in the choir, and how I'd tried to train my children to be reverent in his house. I then asked for his special help that day that the children would behave, and particularly that the child I had with me would sit quietly. The Lord heard my prayer. I never had to leave a meeting once while I was singing in the choir. During meetings if the children were hard to handle I would utter a silent prayer, seeking the Lord's help in teaching them to be reverent.

Training three children at once to be reverent was quite a problem. We always had to rely on someone else to help hold a baby. We didn't feel that we could insist that they stick to our methods of keeping the child quiet—especially since they hadn't worked at it during the week. As a result, whichever child sat with someone else usually ended up with something to play with, which created a problem with the other two. We tried to switch the children around so the helping third party usually got a different baby to hold.

During this time, we found it especially appropriate to handle reverence problems during family home evening. We could easily take time then to be firm and talk to the children without it being embarrassing or disturbing. It didn't hurt to stop a lesson momentarily while reinforcing the reverence program.

This training worked so well that we could take eight children to church—ages one through seven—and have them all sit on the bench quietly throughout an entire meeting. Many people commented on how easy it seemed for them to sit there and how reverent they all were. I thought, If they only knew all the hours that had gone into training them to be that way. As my brother had said, "It doesn't just happen, you have to work at it."

I remember when the triplets were old enough to go into the Relief Society nursery. Occasionally, on homemaking day, I would stay late to help quilt. At these times I picked the triplets up from the nursery and put them each on a chair, telling them to sit there and not get down. They sat by me till I was through quilting. The Relief Society president commented to me how amazed she was that they never got down, and I didn't have to remind them. They weren't the docile, quiet type, but they had been trained.

However, there were days when the children were older that even I wondered if I had ever trained them to be reverent. There were times when I wanted to go up during a meeting and tap them on the shoulder to remind them as they sat with the deacons or in their respective Sunday School classes. I refrained because I didn't want to embarrass them publicly until I had reminded them privately. Besides, I could still remember how difficult on various occasions it had been for me to remain perfectly quiet and reverent.

I know that it is possible to train our little ones to be reverent in the Lord's house. I sincerely believe he will assist us in this program if we will only enlist his help. So we mustn't give up. We only fail when we quit trying.

Chapter 5

Slave or Bookworm

During the first few years of our marriage I had the privilege of living next door to the cleanest neighbor anyone could ever have. She was a perfect example, and it was a great challenge for me to try to keep my home half as clean as hers.

I took mental note of all the things she did. She scrubbed and waxed every floor in her house three to four times a week. She also washed down her walls each week, and hosed down the patio and porches several times as well. Her house was immaculate, to say the least. Her four children could play on any floor in light-colored pajamas and nightgowns and keep spotlessly clean.

My great desire was to have a house as shiny and sparkling as hers. Fridays became my work—or, more aptly put, "slave"—day. A typical Friday began very early in the morning when I cleaned out all of my kitchen cupboards. Then I tackled the refrigerator and stove. Defrosting the refrigerator took quite some time, as there weren't frost-free ones in those days, but it had to be done. Over the years I had become quite fanatical about clean stoves and ovens. I found it was just as easy to keep them clean as dirty. As a result, cleaning my stove was never a huge job on Fridays. Finally, my kitchen walls had to be washed down, and the kitchen floor scrubbed and waxed. After doing this, I always carefully spread newspapers or a sheet of plastic where the children might spill and undo all my hard work.

From the kitchen I went to the bathroom and scoured and cleaned everything there and then scrubbed and waxed that floor. The bedrooms were next (thank goodness we only had two). There were hardwood floors in each that I dusted and buffed; then I dusted the walls and wiped off the dirty marks.

Next the living room had to be done. I pulled out all the furniture from the walls and vacuumed thoroughly and then washed each wall. After pushing the furniture back I vacuumed the upholstery and the rug, then cleaned and polished all the wood furniture. Finally I cleaned the windows and doors.

Last of all came the porches, which had to be swept and hosed off, and then the basement stairs had to be swept and scrubbed.

I went through this ritual each and every Friday for years, always ending up thoroughly exhausted. I got so I hated Fridays to come, but still I continued with each task. I even chided myself that I didn't scrub and wax all the floors four times a week as my neighbor did. Her basement was finished too, so she had more floors to do. No matter how hard I worked my house never seemed to be as clean and neat as hers.

It almost seemed as though the children knew when Fridays had arrived. They always seemed to be more mischievous and to cause more problems. (Could it possibly have been they were getting less attention?) I finally resorted to taking them to the drive-in in the afternoon for an ice cream cone and sometimes a hamburger too, if finances would permit. This saved my kitchen floor a while longer, and helped pacify the children.

After working so hard to get the house clean, I couldn't really let the children relax and live in it for a few days, or it seemed so worthless. Those first few spills on the kitchen floor each week really upset me. And handprints on the wall—couldn't children ever learn not to put their dirty hands all over the door and windows and walls? Sometimes I felt they deliberately tried to undo all my hard work.

On Saturdays I went shopping while my husband "watched" the children. Gerald would let the kids amuse themselves, and from the looks of the house you would have thought it hadn't been cleaned for a week. Seeing my discouragement after a few such Saturday trips, he finally made the children sit on the couch the whole time I was gone. I wasn't happy about that either, but he'd remind me that at least the house was still clean.

Fortunately, Gerald was quite resourceful, and soon became adept at inventing games and stories to keep the children occupied and happy while I was gone. Lunch time was especially unusual, as he made a game out of it. He would line all the children up either on the table or on the counter. He used one pan to warm up leftovers or soup. Then, using one spoon, he proceeded to feed them one spoonful each, going down the line and occasionally interspersing a drink of milk (out of one glass) with the food. Each child was eager for his turn, and no one ever turned a spoonful down. Afterwards they each got a cookie to eat outside or at the table or counter so there were no crumbs on the floor. The cleanup was easy, there were no picky eaters, and everyone was happy.

I put myself through so many agonies in those early years that I could have avoided easily if I had been a little wiser. When the first set of twins started getting around on their own, I moved all my plants out of reach. Then my mother commented one day while visiting us that she had never had to move anything up when her children were little. Determined not to be outdone by my mother, I moved all the plants back into reach. I must have vacuumed up dirt from tipped-over plants at least three times a day for the next six months.

My nerves got very bad as I tried to clean up after all the messes these first twins created. They worked together at everything. I could be in the kitchen working, and I'd hear them start to unroll the toilet paper in the bathroom. By the time I'd reach them, they'd nearly always have most of it unwound. One would cram the paper into the toilet bowl as fast as the other could unroll it. Their teamwork was unusual for children so young.

One Friday I showered and changed clothes after doing my usual cleaning, and then took a minute to enjoy my clean house and the new wallpaper we had put up in the kitchen the week before. The wallpaper wasn't washable, but it added such a special touch to our kitchen that we had put it up anyway. After surveying the scene with satisfaction, I ran outside to turn the water on the lawn. I couldn't have been gone more than two or three minutes. When I returned to the kitchen, I couldn't believe my eyes. My lovely wallpaper was plastered with shortening. In the middle of the kitchen floor honey, shortening, sugar, flour, and powdered milk had been all dumped together and strewn around. In the middle of it all sat my twins, gleefully licking their fingers and kicking the conglomeration around. Poor Beckie was telling them no and trying to pick up the sugar and return it to the right container. I couldn't believe my eyes, and I figured no one else would either, so I got the camera and took a picture. We have laughed over it many times since, but tears were closer to the surface when it happened.

By the time my second twins were old enough to get around on their own, I had become a little wiser. I came to the conclusion that I wasn't the same as my mother, and neither had her situation been the same as mine. My plants, due to the mistreatment they received from the first twins had long since been gone, and I hadn't replaced them. With a few guilty feelings of not quite measuring up, I had moved my other nice things out of the reach of little hands. Little by little my house had become more childproof, and my nerves had had a chance to calm down somewhat. But I wasn't ready to give up my attempts at a clean house, so my Friday rituals continued. I was always disappointed that my house never seemed to measure up to those right around me.

As I mentally tore myself apart, I never seemed to realize that there was a positive side of the scale as well as a negative. In accounting class in college I had learned all about debits and credits and how they had to balance, but I failed to apply that principle in my life. I saw only the good things my neighbors accomplished and compared myself in the same areas, without looking at the whole picture honestly.

For instance, I had five small children and my neighbor had four older children spaced further apart. I was very active in the Church—attending many meetings and fulfilling my calling as Laurel teacher besides being a visiting teacher, singing in the choir and Relief Society Chorus, and attending the rehearsals for each group. My husband was active in the elders quorum and served as president during some of this time. I also sewed most of my family's clothes, knitted their sweaters, and made most of the gifts we gave away. If I had taken time to see things in their proper perspective, I would have seen on the positive side of my scale all the things that didn't appear on my neighbor's. Her husband wasn't a member of the Church. She frequently went to meetings with her children, but she didn't always hold a position. She didn't own a sewing machine, and so she didn't make all the other things I did. Yet she was perhaps the best Christian I have ever met. She was always there when I needed help, and my children loved to be in her home as much as they did their own.

Because I was so critical of myself, I failed to see the good things I was able to accomplish. This created an unrest in me to which my whole family seemed to react negatively. First of all, it was very frustrating to me to work so hard and to have it seem so unappreciated, as shown, for example, in my husband's not keeping the house clean for me while I was shopping. Also, the children seemed to be so careless; this made me cross, and they reacted to my crossness. All this work that I imposed on myself brought me nothing much in return but a few moments of satisfaction and a bunch of frayed nerves. Still I continued the ritual for years.

I guess the Lord saw me in a hopeless plight and decided to help me out of the pit I had dug for myself. One year we had an unusually excellent Relief Society teacher named Ora Liston. I shall never forget the lesson she gave that changed my life. She had been talking about our homes, and told how she had become a slave to her house, even though she only had one child. One day she sat and took stock of herself and said, "Ora, you can't take this clean house with you when you die. All you're going to be able to take is what you store up here"—and she pointed to her head. She told us how this had changed her life. She said she still tried to keep her house clean, but now you might see a few books or other clutter around when you came to her house. She had started a program of storing up knowledge. I was really impressed by her lesson—not just with the words she was saying, but with a special spirit that seemed to carry the message right to my heart. In my patriarchal blessing I had been told to fill my mind with useful information for the mission of instructing souls in the paths of righteousness.

I went away from that lesson imbued with determination to make changes in my life. My Friday rituals were altered. Some things were done other days in the week and some things were done not nearly so often. I never really got over wishing my home would look more like my neighbors', but I realized I had more important things to accomplish.

My whole attitude seemed to change. I was more relaxed, and my husband and children all seemed to be happier. I spent more time studying the gospel—at least an hour a day now. My spirit began to be fed and nourished. My testimony grew stronger, and I spent a great deal more time meditating on the gospel and spiritual things. The Lord seemed so much closer, and I became more aware of his great sacrifice and love for me. I seemed to have been blessed with a change of heart—a new spirit. My only intent and desire was to serve the Lord. I loved him as I had never loved him before, and he became my whole life. I wanted to do only as he would have me do.

What a special time that was in my life! It was glorious, and I have reflected often since that it only came after I quit being a slave to my house and became more interested in learning of the Lord's ways and trying to serve him better.

Chapter 6

Some Special Help

Having two and three babies at a time posed some real problems in our lives. Thanks to the help of our Father in heaven, we were able to make it through a number of tests of our endurance, our health, and our willingness to pull together as a family.

When Gerald and I went to tithing settlement while I was pregnant with Kerry and Kyle, we had a very special experience. I didn't think anyone even knew I was pregnant. Five times during the interview the bishop asked me how my health was. I kept telling him I was fine. When we got up to go, he told us how blessings of the priesthood can save the lives of little children and babies. He told us there had been occasions right in our own ward when the priesthood had been called upon and a baby's life had been spared. I thought it a little strange that the bishop was telling us all this, but I didn't dwell on it. In fact, I forgot all about it until a few months later.

I had been to the doctor for a checkup. He suspected another multiple birth and had sent me to be x-rayed. When I returned to his office, the call came that confirmed his suspicions: I was carrying two again. He warned me that I would have to be very careful because there would be no chance of saving them unless I carried them at least another month. I had three small children at home, and he warned me about lifting them or doing anything that might bring on premature contractions.

A few days later I was fixing breakfast for the children. Gerald had already left for work. Suddenly I felt that familiar pain in my lower back and felt my stomach hardening. Panic washed over me as I struggled hard to untangle my frenzied thoughts. Somehow I managed to make it into the living room and onto the recliner chair.

I called Beckie to help me. She was only four, but seemed to sense the gravity of the situation. I asked her to help Debbie and Eric with their breakfast and to try to clean up the kitchen for me. I don't know how we managed, but somehow Beckie was able to take care of the twins for me throughout the day. I don't know why I didn't send her to a neighbor for help. It seemed all I could think about was that day in the bishop's office and his words of counsel to me. I kept praying that the labor wouldn't get too hard till Gerald returned from work.

I spent the whole day reclining in the chair, not daring to move for fear of bringing on hard labor. Finally 5 o'clock came, and Gerald arrived home. I apprised him quickly of the situation and asked him to call Bishop Russon. The bishop came and gave me a blessing. The labor ceased before he left and didn't return until five weeks before the babies were due. The boys were born well and healthy, weighing in at seven pounds one ounce and six pounds three ounces. They were good sized for being five weeks early; the Lord had shown forth his hand in our lives again.

I have reflected often on that experience and the marvelous inspiration our bishop had received in counseling us. I was so young and inexperienced that I'm sure I would have lost the babies if the Lord hadn't stepped in and prompted our bishop.

This wasn't the only time the Lord interceded in our behalf. When I was two months pregnant with the triplets, I started hemorrhaging one Saturday night. We called the doctor, and he told me to go to bed. Then we called Bishop Russon, and he came over and administered to me. Before he did, he explained that if it were a healthy pregnancy he would bless me that it would be saved; if it weren't healthy, this was nature's way of releasing it and we shouldn't interfere. Then he and my husband administered to me.

The following Thursday I was still hemorrhaging. My mother came over and was quite concerned. She suggested we call the doctor again because she was afraid I would bleed to death. The doctor was very shocked that I hadn't lost the pregnancy. He told my husband to bring me right in. After examining me, the doctor walked out of the room shaking his head. His nurse returned with him, and he examined me again. "There's no reason for her not losing it," he told the nurse. Wondering what was going on, I raised my head, intent on asking one question: "Is the pregnancy healthy?"

The doctor looked at me and shook his head again. "I can't understand why you haven't lost it," he said, "but everything appears to be all right." I lay back down and relaxed, even though he was cautioning me. I knew all would be well.

My blood was dangerously low, and I needed an immediate transfusion. However, the doctor didn't want to give me one for fear of doing anything out of the ordinary that might possibly dislodge the pregnancy. He finally decided to let me see if I couldn't build my blood back up on my own. He sent me home and confined me to bed.

The true Christian character of my next-door neighbor was really portrayed to me during this time. She came over each morning with her two daughters, and they went completely through my house and cleaned it and did my laundry. She took the ironing home and either took the children with them or left the girls to tend them. This went on for two weeks before the Relief Society sisters came in and rescued my neighbor from a somewhat permanent job. I remember distinctly how guilty I felt at having to have someone else take over my responsibilities.

The Relief Society president came early every morning. She got things organized and either took my children with her or sent someone else to come and stay at our home during the day. Many women in our ward just dropped by and helped out, independent of a Relief Society assignment. We had so much food brought in and so many different people helping us that I began feeling guilty.

I had never had so much kindness showered upon me. I really appreciated all the help, and yet I felt so guilty and so helpless. I was quite discouraged. My brother-in-law, who was serving as a bishop at the time, noticed my despondency and asked me about it. When he finally got me to admit what was bothering me, I felt relieved. I knew he'd sympathize with me and understand.

His understanding was much greater than I anticipated—but it also went in a totally different direction than I had expected. He asked me why I thought all these sisters were coming to help me every day. I was so concerned about myself that I hadn't looked at it from their side. He then asked me what I would do if the situation were reversed and one of them was confined to bed. Why, I would go and help, of course. Then he said something to me that struck me so deeply I have never forgotten it. He said, "Would you deprive them of a blessing?"

He let me understand that I might possibly be an instrument in the Lord's hands to build a strong spiritual bond in these sisters through the service they were rendering.

That summer seemed eternally long. I was such an active person that it was very difficult for me to be in bed. I finally talked my husband into bringing my sewing machine into the bedroom. He put it by the side of my bed, and I was able to work it with one hand guiding the fabric and one hand working the power. At least I was still able to make my children's clothing.

The weeks passed, and it would soon be time for Mutual to begin. I was the Laurel teacher. The Mutual president had been to see me several times. She told me the mother of one of the new Laurels had asked if I were going to be able to teach. Her daughter had been waiting for two years to get into my class. I loved those girls so much that I desperately wanted to keep the class. When I found out someone wanted me for a teacher, I was more determined than ever that somehow I would teach .

The bishopric came to see me and to talk about my class. They suggested getting a substitute until I could get on my feet. (I had been hemorrhaging for over two months.) I begged them to let me keep my class even if I had to teach the girls from my bed. The bishop told me that if I were that determined, they'd have to see that I got well.

The week came for Mutual to start, and I was still in bed. I prepared my lesson and prayed that I'd be able to get up. I asked Gerald to call the doctor and ask for permission for me to go teach my class. The doctor said I could go to the church to give my lesson if I would sit in a chair propped up with pillows. I was not to stand to present the lesson, and I had to go directly home and to bed afterward. Also I was to go to his office for a checkup first thing the next morning.

How exuberant I was! My class was truly understanding and considerate. There was a rich outpouring of the Spirit that night. Two stake leaders attended the class; both were from our ward, and one was a nurse. I didn't think about it then, but they were probably there in case I needed help. At any rate, they both felt the Spirit there, and it was a lovely occasion.

December arrived. I had been up and around somewhat for two months but still wasn't able to completely care for my household. Since my activities were so restricted, my mother came to help every day.

When I went to the doctor for my weekly checkup, he told me that if I didn't carry these babies for another three weeks at least, I'd never save them. I went home a little concerned and reported to my mother what he had said.

"Okay," she said, "back to bed you go."

"He didn't tell me to go to bed," I objected. But there was no persuading my mother. For three weeks, every time I even stirred on the bed, she was checking up on me. I had had several contractions a day for four months, and she wasn't taking any chances that they'd turn into real labor prematurely.

On December 17 the three weeks were up. Early the next morning, I was in the hospital, and our three little miracle babies were born. There were only six minutes between the first birth and the last one, but even then the delivery had been hard on the third baby, Wendy. Her lungs didn't expand as they should have; there was a hollow in her chest.

Gerald was working part-time to help boost our finances, so he couldn't come to see me that night of the triplets' birth, but my parents came during visiting hours. I told them about Wendy's condition. My mother gently told me that the purpose of this life had been fulfilled. Wendy's spirit had come to earth and received a body. I heard her, but I also calmly asked her to go call Bishop Russon.

Bishop Russon called a member of the high council, and they came to the hospital that evening, a Friday. The triplets were in incubators in an isolated nursery. Before the two men could go in and administer to Wendy, the nurses scrubbed them practically from head to toe and put sterile gowns on them. They went in and did the administering through holes in the side of the incubator.

When my pediatrician came in to see me on Monday morning, he told me Wendy had continually improved since Friday night. Somehow I knew and had known that all would be well with her.

Three weeks later when we finally got to take the triplets home, Dr. Snow cautioned me about their care. They were to be kept isolated for two months. Even I didn't realize how difficult that was going to be. People that I didn't even know came to see them, and we had to explain that even our own children couldn't go into the nursery. The doctor told me that if the babies caught cold in their delicate condition, it would be disastrous.

Despite all our precautions, I caught cold. All the sleepless nights I had spent were catching up with me. A nurse in our ward came and gave us all shots except the six-week-old triplets, on instructions from our doctor. Still, Wendy caught cold. It had been two days since she had eaten well. My mother came over to help me, and when she picked Wendy up, she quickly surmised the situation and called to me. She told me the baby was dying, and I'd better get hold of my doctor. Gerald had just left for work. I didn't even hesitate but went right in and called Bishop Russon. He brought a member of our bishopric and came right over.

I don't remember the particulars of the blessing except that I had a very special feeling, and that he promised Wendy she would grow to womanhood. That was such a special occasion in our lives that I shed many tears then and have shed many tears since as I realized how greatly blessed by the Lord we have been.

After bringing the triplets home, I found myself in a situation in which I couldn't handle everything myself—a real shock to my system. But I had learned from my long confinement, so I didn't wallow in self-pity. Instead I took a close look at my situation and tried to figure out ways of solving my problems.

First of all, I had three babies who required most of my attention. They had been born two months premature and needed extra care. The doctor had kept them in the hospital for three weeks trying to get their weight up to five pounds. I remember well the morning he called and told me two of them had reached five pounds and the third was just a couple of ounces under. Then he said I could take one or two of them or even all three if I wanted. I quickly replied that I would take all three. He laughed and said, "I rather thought you would."

We were all really excited to bring the triplets home. The children were eager to see these new sisters they had heard so much about. Beckie was six, Debbie and Eric were four, Kerry and Kyle were two. Add three premature babies to that group, and I really had my hands full.

I soon found that it took me about an hour to feed each baby (if they didn't throw up, which they did quite regularly). So it usually took me three hours to feed them, and if I was lucky, the first one would sleep for about half an hour after I finished feeding the last one before I had to start all over again. This left me just enough time occasionally to throw something together for the other children to eat and perhaps to put a batch of wash in. If a baby threw up during her feeding, this threw me off schedule, and I lost my half-hour break.

After a few weeks of not being able to clean my house (thank goodness I'd already given up my Friday cleaning rituals) and not being able to keep up with the laundry or fix anything but jiffy meals, I knew something had to give.

Beckie had always been very good to help with the other children, and I had relied on her a great deal those first few weeks the triplets were home. But even with all her efforts, I knew I was never going to make it. I needed some special help. So I went to the Lord and told him my situation and asked for help in solving my problem.

There was no immediate answer to my prayer, but I'm sure the Lord guided and prompted me as I set about organizing our household. Beckie was the supervisor over the older children, and fixed their breakfast and lunch. We taught her how to use the washing machine and dryer so she could put clothes in for me.

Debbie became the chief diaper changer, and it wasn't long till she could change a diaper as well as most adults. She loved babies and was a natural at this job. She also helped Beckie with the breakfast and lunch and folded the mountains of diapers we used. If I couldn't get the rest of the laundry folded, she and Beckie took care of that as well. Between the two of them, and with Eric's help occasionally, they managed the vacuuming for me.

Eric was the head dishwasher. He pulled a chair over to the sink (we didn't have a dishwasher in those days) and washed all the dishes and then moved the chair and dried them. He was really tiny to be doing such a big job, and I can picture him yet at that sink with dishwater up to his elbows because the sink was so deep for his small body. He carefully picked up one dish at a time, washed it, and turned it over to inspect it. Then he carefully rinsed it—using both hands—and leaned way over to place it in the drainer.

The older three children were assigned to make their own beds and helped their two younger brothers make theirs. Whoever was the least busy did the dusting. They helped each other in the remaining jobs I needed done—such as sweeping floors and porches and cleaning sinks.

Kerry and Kyle always brought the diapers to me and were

so good to run errands and help pick up around the house. Little children love to play fifty-pick-up—a simple game in which each person picks up fifty things off the floor. Some items were things needing to be put away; some were just plain clutter that needed to be thrown away. Sometimes there were a lot of lint pieces from the laundry that needed picking off the carpet. The children thought it was a fun game. They didn't realize they were working (and learning to count at the same time!). Often they would be the instigators and say it was time to play fifty-pick-up.

There was a special spirit in our home. Each child felt important and a part of the family team. They all felt needed, and work didn't seem like work to them—it was more of a game.

People were amazed at how much our children did and how well they handled their jobs. A local newspaper reporter came and interviewed us and wrote an article on our family. She asked me how I could possibly manage with so many small children. I told her that you simply have to have a system, and that children can work.

Using a little psychology is also helpful. I always sincerely praised the children for what they did and told them how much I appreciated them. I explained to them that I simply couldn't manage without their help. And I never redid the work they had done. I didn't have time to in the first place, but beyond that, it would have killed their spirit and initiative. It was important for them to feel that their work was totally acceptable to me, and it was. I was so grateful for their help, and even if it wasn't always done exactly as I would have done it, there was no way I could have managed without them.

About this time a friend asked me what she could do with her two children. They always seemed to be at each other, or one tormenting the other. After watching the family for a while, I realized her children did none of the work. They weren't nearly as happy as they were after she gave them assignments. Children are much happier when they help and receive praise for their accomplishments. It makes them feel good inside.

As the triplets grew older and required less of my time, I took over the heavier housework from my children. I relieved them of the vacuuming, scrubbing the floors, and the laundry. Eric was released as chief dishwasher. He did the breakfast and lunch dishes and his sisters did the dinner dishes. While they did dishes, he fed one of the triplets as Gerald and I fed the other two. The children still helped with much of the work because I had learned that their being included had created a happier atmosphere in our home.

As the children grew older, their work assignments changed. We usually made a list of the jobs that needed doing and let them choose their own. They always chose more than I would have assigned them. When they started school, their job assignments were changed. We rotated the jobs often, since they got tired of doing the same job; besides, they needed to learn how to do many different things. The family home evening before school let out was an opportune time to make up work lists and let them choose their assignments. They all took part and helped make the list of jobs to be done. Then each child chose one job and waited till all the others chose one before he selected his second and third assignments. It seemed more fair that way.

Children can do and will offer to do many things if they are included in the planning. Right now the triplets are thirteen, and they have made all the bread for our family for over a year. We don't have an electric bread mixer—they don't make them large enough for our family—so the girls use a hand one and their older brothers help them with the kneading.

There are always jobs that no one wants to do, but each child has to take his turn with these. The system works out better if the distasteful assignments are rotated fairly often. Of course, if the children don't do their work well, they have to continue to perform that particular function until they have learned how to do it. They soon learn that if they don't like a job, they're better off doing it the best they can so they can hurry and get a change of assignments.

Through all of our experience we have learned why the Lord counseled us to "cease to be idle." People (including children) are so much better natured and happier when they're busy. We have really found out that a happy home is a busy home.

Chapter 7

Organizing, Teaching, and Planning

If we want to accomplish something, we must set goals. If goals are to be met, we have to plan. Then our plans must be set in order of priority so we can get first things done first. This is a good basic rule, but as with most rules we have to allow for exceptions. Even if we plan well and set priorities, inopportune situations sometimes occur that undo even the best of plans. If we don't realize this at the outset, we may tend to get discouraged.

Suppose I have organized and planned well. My day starts off in a disaster. The children won't eat. They play in their food and before I know it, there's cereal and milk on my clean floor and all over them. By the time I get them, their clothes, and the kitchen cleaned up, I'm already behind our planned schedule. Then the phone rings—not once, not twice, but several times during the day. The baby cries early, friends drop by to visit, and so the day goes—entirely apart from my plans. At the end of the day, I think over my planned schedule and am reduced to tears because I've accomplished a total zero. But that's negative thinking; Satan is trying to discourage me. We shouldn't be so quick to chastise ourselves, thinking we've accomplished nothing. Instead, we should add up the things we did do even if they weren't on our schedule. It may be surprising how much we really did accomplish. At any rate, tomorrow is another day and today is past. We can't change what has already happened today, but our attitude toward tomorrow could have a great deal of effect on how much we accomplish tomorrow. A mother has so many responsibilities that she needs to achieve to the maximum of her potential each day.

One of the main responsibilities a mother has is to teach and train her children. I was determined to do the very best I could in this regard. First of all, I decided my children must be taught the scriptures. I started teaching Beckie from the Book of Mormon when she was about three. I would open my book and, glancing at it occasionally, I would tell her in words I thought she could understand what was in the chapter. We went through one chapter each day. I was most faithful at doing this and felt quite strongly that it was my duty. We had covered First and Second Nephi when my sister, who is excellent with little children, came over for a visit. She listened while I finished the chapter, then looked at me for a minute and said, "Janice, I don't know how to tell you this, but she didn't understand a word you said." I stared at her in utter disbelief. "I didn't read it from the book," I said, feeling somewhat dejected. I should have realized that since I was trained to teach high school students, and really had no interest in teaching small children, I wouldn't be able to relate to them easily. I asked my sister what I should do, but she didn't solve my problem. That weekend I went to a bookstore and looked through the children's books. How delighted I was to find a book by Emma Marr Petersen, *Book of Mormon Stories*, and especially to find that it was based on doctrine. I went home armed with my new teaching aid. What a joy it was to see Beckie's interest as we read the book each day. Later we purchased Sister Petersen's *Bible Stories* and *Stories from the History of Our Church*. I read to the children each morning during breakfast. They loved the books, and as we finished one we started on another.

Our morning ritual changed somewhat when Beckie entered junior high and had to leave earlier for school. As the children reached that age, I encouraged them to read the scriptures on their own. How exciting it was for me to walk into my nine-year-old son's bedroom and find him lying on his bed deeply engrossed in the Book of Mormon, and to see him at sixteen enjoying the Old Testament over a huge bowl of homemade granola. Or to see his twin sister (at seventeen) read all the standard works in eight months.

Family home evening is also a great aid in teaching the children the gospel. When they were younger, they were delighted to take turns presenting the lessons. We really encouraged this because the teacher always learns more than the people being taught. I was continually amazed at their ingenuity: they really presented the lessons better to each other than I would have done. My husband also gave excellent lessons, but I always felt that mine didn't go over very well.

When the older five became teenagers, our family home evenings weren't as successful. My husband and I discussed the problem quite a bit and tried several different approaches. Nothing seemed to work. Most of the older children no longer wanted to teach the lessons—a couple of them could be persuaded occasionally but generally didn't want to. If the younger children presented a lesson, they were heckled by their older brothers and sisters. Our family home evenings were anything but ideal in those days.

Something had to be done, but what? It seemed we had tried everything. Then one day my husband read in one of the older manuals a suggestion that for our type of family it was sometimes effective to divide into two groups. Nothing else had worked, so we decided to try this. We presented the plan to the children and they agreed unanimously. So we separated: I took the older five children, and my husband took the four younger ones. We met together for treats afterward.

The new plan worked beautifully. The younger children now were taking turns presenting the lessons. The older children still didn't want to teach, and as I experimented with different lessons, I was still getting only a mediocre response. After praying about it, I decided to go into some deeper doctrine and teach my children as I would teach seventeen- or eighteen-year-olds. My lessons were successful again. One of my more outspoken boys was quick to tell me which type of lesson would bring a favorable response. Young people know what they like, and my task was much easier when I was appealing to their interests. I was amazed at how much more advanced they were in gospel knowledge than I had been at the same age. I have applied teacher development principles in my lessons, giving the children challenges to try to help them grow spiritually as well as doctrinally, and they have responded well. Occasionally they ask for an activity night, or maybe for a short lesson when they have a great deal of homework. I have even condescended to watching Monday night football for an activity. It's not family home evening in the true sense if we're trying to pound things into the family that they are in no mood to receive. There needs to be a congenial spirit, even if it means we have to compromise occasionally. Remember, it wasn't the Lord's way to force.

To further teach gospel principles and doctrine to the children, we invested in some gospel-oriented games. These were the type that asked questions and gave points or moves for correct answers. Some of the questions were too difficult for the children at first, but they enjoyed our being together and playing anyway. We gave them clues when they didn't know the answers, and if that didn't help, we gave them three choices, one of which was the correct answer.

I also invented one of my own games. It started out being "Book of Mormon Questions." When the children were still quite small, I asked them questions about the reading we had done from *Book of Mormon Stories.* This game soon became a Sunday afternoon pastime. I'd direct a question to one child; if that child couldn't answer it, then anyone could try. Sometimes I'd just ask a general question for them all to answer. I was really amazed at how much the children retained.

On one occasion when we were playing, my oldest son seemed to know all the answers. So when it was his turn for an individual question, I asked a more difficult one. This went on, and he continued to answer all questions given to him. He began acting a little too smug after quickly answering a difficult question, so I threw another one out quickly that I knew would stump him. I said, "Okay, name the four sons of Mosiah."

"Ammon, Aaron, Omner, and Himni," he quickly said.

I nearly fell off the chair in shock, but controlled myself so as to not let him know I was surprised. I threw another one out. "Name the three sons of Alma the younger."

"Helaman, Shiblon, and Corianton."

I was visibly stunned then. I have wished many times since that I had asked him to name the three sons of King Benjamin—just to see if he could have done it. He was about seven years old at the time.

This game that started with the *Book of Mormon* has continued to be a family favorite. When we have been traveling a long time and the children become restless, it has been a lifesaver. We've played it while we've been camping, picnicking, and traveling. We still play it, but now it's "gospel questions." My fifteen-year-old son wanted to play it after our last family home evening. The children never seem to grow too old for it or get tired of it. Now that they're older, they give me questions sometimes too. Increasing their knowledge wasn't the primary purpose here, but rather creating an interest in spiritual matters.

Teaching the children household duties and motivating them to complete the tasks as I desired was a somewhat different challenge. The older children had had to learn many things on their own without a proper period of learning and instruction. When they were younger I had accepted and praised what they had done because they had done the best they knew how, and I truly appreciated their help.

When my schedule relaxed somewhat, I had opportunity to teach them the proper way. I learned that we can't expect children to complete a job to our satisfaction if we don't explain exactly what we expect and make certain they understand what we're saying. Too often parents assume that children understand, forgetting that little ones don't always comprehend adult language.

I heard a story once in a teacher development course that really drove this point home. A three-year-old boy had wandered away from home and ventured clear to the corner by the time his father found him. The father took the boy home and told him not to go to the corner or he'd get spanked. A while later the boy was missing again. The father found him down at the corner. The father spanked him and returned him home. He again told the little boy not to go to the corner or he'd get spanked. Well, the little boy ventured off again, was found at the corner, received his spanking, was returned home, and was warned about the corner again. This visit to the corner was repeated several times during the day and so were the spankings. About the tenth time they returned from the corner, the father was quite upset and told the boy once more, "Now, don't go to the corner again or you'll get spanked." The little boy sobbed, "Wwwwwwhat's tthe cccorner?" Then the father realized the boy hadn't once really understood what was being said to him.

As parents we mustn't assume that children understand. We must carefully explain things to them using words that they can clearly understand. I believe that many times children are punished when in reality they aren't at fault, because they haven't understood adult terminology.

I spent time with each child showing him how to do a job, and then let him do it. While they were little, the children seemed to enjoy the work more and did a better job. When they got older, it seemed that their interest died down and their work wasn't as acceptable.

For example, when they finished the dishes, they failed to thoroughly clean around the sink and shine the chrome. Sometimes the stove didn't look like it had been cleaned at all. When

I'd send the children to clean their rooms, they would reappear much too soon to have done a thorough job. Their idea of clean certainly wasn't mine. I don't know if they were being lazy or if they truly didn't know what I expected. All of these things were a source of irritation to me. I knew something had to be done.

I sat down and made out cards with checklists of steps I expected the children to complete for each job. For example, on the *After Bath* card would appear steps such as:

1. Drain water
2. Rinse and wash out tub
3. Clean out soap tray
4. Shine chrome
5. Hang up washcloth
6. Hang up towel straight
7. Put dirty clothes in hamper
8. Remove all your things from the bathroom

It was amazing how much they improved. When they told me they had completed a job, before I'd go to check I would ask if they had completed everything on the checklist. Sometimes they decided to go read it again and make sure before I checked. The checklists not only improved the children's techniques, but they saved a lot of frayed nerves and hurt feelings. They also helped me to be a much more patient mother.

I had always been very interested in all the homemaking arts and crafts, and I wanted my daughters to be interested in them too. My sister-in-law had been raised in Germany, and she had told me how she learned to knit before she went to school. It was hard to believe that a child so young could learn to do such a thing. I had been taught to knit by an English girl the summer I was fifteen, and I remember how awkward it had been for me to hold the needles and make all the correct motions. I dropped many a stitch while I was learning.

I pondered on these things for a while before I decided I'd tackle teaching my five-year-old how to knit. I knew my talents lay in teaching teenagers, not small children. My first attempts at teaching the gospel to my children had not been too successful, so I started on this new teaching venture with more than a little hesitancy.

I got my knitting needles and some yarn and called Beckie in. We sat on the couch, and I told her it was time for her to learn to knit. (I didn't ask her if she wanted to learn because if she had said no, I would have dropped it and rationalized that I had tried anyway.) Much to my amazement she was quite eager to learn how. She had watched me as I had made many baby things, and she wanted to make things for her dolls.

We were all set to begin when Debbie walked in, surveyed the situation, and said, "I want to learn too." She promptly climbed up on the couch and sat on the other side of me. I really wasn't prepared for that. Debbie was not yet four years old. I didn't want to stop any desire for learning that she had, but how was I possibly going to teach a three-year-old to knit? I couldn't think of any way out, so I handed her two needles and some yarn.

They both handled the casting-on process without too much difficulty. I thought that was quite enough to learn for one day, but they didn't. They wanted to be able to use both needles. I heaved a big sigh, knowing there was no direction to go now but forward. I had started something, and I was determined to finish it.

Can you imagine my surprise when Debbie caught on almost immediately? It was more difficult for Beckie, and I had to keep encouraging her so she wouldn't give up. They each worked on a small swatch and did straight knitting. When they had mastered that technique well, I taught them how to purl, which was more difficult. Debbie's tension was remarkable. I was so amazed at her ability that I saved her first two samplers, the one on which she did straight knitting and another on which she learned to purl.

When I was confined to bed before the triplets arrived, I did a lot of knitting. Debbie used to climb on the bed beside me and knit away. The Relief Society sisters would watch her in utter disbelief, saying they wouldn't have believed it if they hadn't seen it themselves. By the time Debbie was five, she had knit each of her younger brothers a pair of slippers.

All of the girls were taught to knit and crochet before they went to school. The younger ones have not done it as much as the older ones—probably because I haven't done nearly as much myself—but they all know how.

The summer after Beckie reached nine, I decided it was time to teach her to sew. I wasn't shocked this time when Debbie tagged along. I merely wondered if I had patience enough to teach both a nine-year-old and a seven-year-old. I started them off on an easy apron. I taught them how to pull threads to get a straight cut. We didn't use a pattern, so I taught them how to measure off a length big enough for apron, waistband, and ties. That part wasn't too difficult. We had a lesson on the use and care of the sewing machine. I also taught them about sewing scissors and shears. All of the children knew better than to use any of my sewing scissors for cutting anything but fabric. I didn't know about using lined paper and no thread in the machine to teach them how to sew straight. One of the girls learned that method later in a home economics class and used it to teach her sisters how to sew straight.

We finished the aprons before summer was over, and the girls wanted to make something else, but I wasn't game. I told them we'd make nightgowns the following summer. For the present they could practice on doll clothes.

Again, Debbie was a natural. She had sat by me often as I sewed, but after that first summer of instruction she became almost like my shadow. As a result, when I taught them to make nightgowns the following summer, she had a fairly easy time. Setting in the sleeve proved to be no problem for her, but it was difficult for Beckie. I soon learned that I could explain something and Debbie would catch on immediately, whereas Beckie never seemed to understand my instructions. Sometimes I'd just plain give up, thinking I'd never be able to teach her—then Debbie would explain it to her, and she'd be able to do it. By the time Debbie was twelve, she had started designing and making creations of her own. She was also making many things for her little sisters.

The summer Debbie was twelve, one of my friends called and asked if I'd teach her daughter how to sew. She wanted to pay me for giving her lessons. I didn't really have the time or the inclination, so I offered Debbie's services instead. My friend accepted, and Debbie started giving sewing lessons. She was truly kind and understanding and had a great deal of patience—entirely different from what I would have been.

Beckie was making most of her own clothes too, though she said it was more because she wanted the clothes than because she enjoyed the sewing. However, she kept at it, and has learned to look at a dress and be able to copy it without a pattern. Debbie's achievements came through natural ability, while Beckie had to work at it, but they both have achieved, and that is the important thing.

These older two girls have helped greatly in teaching their younger sisters. Tanya, our ninth and youngest child, was making all kinds of purses and doll clothes at age seven. The triplets at age twelve made most of their own school clothes—pants with pockets and zippers, and tops to go with them. At age nine, Tanya made her summer shorts and knit tops.

Another homemaking art I wanted the children to learn was cooking. They had helped with the baking from the time they were quite small. All children seem to enjoy making cookies, a small pie when mother makes big ones, a tiny loaf of bread in their play pans when mother bakes bread, or a small cake when mother makes cakes. Our children quickly learned how to make the dough on their own as they neared seven or eight. I think half of the stimulation was that I left them on their own, and they could eat the dough without being reprimanded. I could appreciate that, as I always enjoyed sampling the dough when I was little (and even when I became a mother).

I remember one Saturday when my sister came over to visit. Beckie was eight, Debbie and Eric were six, and Kerry and Kyle were four. They were all in the kitchen making cookies, and I was downstairs sewing. My sister came down and made some comment about my being a good mother to let my children be doing the cooking. I quickly informed her I was downstairs sewing because I couldn't take it. If I had remained in the kitchen, I would have been a nag, and making cookies would no longer be fun to them. Doing it on their own, they learned and had fun without mother heckling them. They knew the rules and cleaned up when they were through.

I had learned that when the children were tackling something that was a little difficult for them, it was best for me to go out of the room. I knew that if I remained, I would just inhibit their progress by overreacting to situations that weren't that serious. What does it hurt if a little flour or sugar gets spilled while little hands are learning?

Of course, in the initial teaching process I had to be there to demonstrate what to do. I had taught Beckie and Debbie how to make a few simple things, such as macaroni and cheese and pancakes, but hadn't ventured much further in teaching them how to cook. Then in a general conference talk Elder S. Dilworth Young spoke about how mothers could better prepare their sons for missions by teaching them how to wash and iron, how to clean, and especially how to cook so they could prepare well-balanced, nourishing meals. I knew I was falling short of what was expected of me, so my husband and I talked it over and decided to institute a new program in our family. We assigned the older five children one weeknight each to fix dinner. I worked with them individually for a few weeks, teaching them how to cook. The children responded well because they were allowed to choose what they wanted to fix, and, of course, they selected their favorites.

After I had spent time teaching them, we decided they could go on their own. Each one was to be responsible for fixing his one meal a week. I was willing to help and offer advice, but it was their responsibility to ask me. They had to plan ahead and get meat out of the freezer themselves. I didn't do anything for them unless they asked me.

This system worked really well at first. Then, after the newness wore off, the children seemed to forget their responsibilities. When dinner time was past and nothing had been fixed, someone would come and ask me when we were going to eat. I'd send them to ask their brother or sister, saying I didn't know. It was surprising how they often truly did forget it was their turn. They'd come to me apologetically and ask what they could fix in a hurry. We ate a lot of hot dogs and macaroni and cheese while they were learning. Sometimes they'd come running in after school having forgotten to take the meat out of the freezer, and we'd end up thawing hamburger while we were cooking it. (We didn't have microwave ovens then.) Through this experience we came up with a lot of ideas for jiffy meals that will help the children while they're on missions or in college.

When I first got married I made a little candy at Christmastime as my mother had always done. I loved beating (and sampling) the fudge and a delicious candy we called "patience" when I was growing up, and I wanted my children to have the same kind of memories. Each year we'd experiment with new recipes, till now making Christmas candy has become a major production at our house. We use twenty pounds of dipping chocolate just to make chocolates. We make a variety of other candies too, including turtles, pecan logs, chews, peanut clusters, cherry-nut bars, patience, fudge (old-fashioned and marshmallow cream), toffee, peanut brittle, caramels, peanut butter cups, and marzipan. The children all make the candy, and the only thing I do anymore is the dipping. Most of the candy is given away to friends, neighbors, and relatives. We also do all kinds of baking—twisties, tea rings, fruit braids, and various other pastries. The children have become quite adept at doing all this, and it brings such togetherness at Christmastime while making gifts for others.

Not all of the household tasks are as enjoyable as cooking. One that seems particularly time-consuming is the shopping. Shopping, I have come to feel, is a necessary time waster. I haven't always felt that way. In the earlier years of our married life, I quite enjoyed it and looked forward to it as a means of getting out of the house. Now that all my children are in school, I begrudge the time I spend shopping. However, it still has to be done.

I have always been a person who has wanted to get the very most I could for my money, so I have had to educate myself on some money-saving processes. Having a very thrifty husband has helped a lot. When we were first married, Gerald was still in college. He took a marketing research class one term, and as a project he decided to do a survey of the grocery stores in the area to find out which ones had the cheapest prices on a particular list of food products. I was delegated to do the legwork for his project. I was very self-conscious walking around grocery stores each week with my food list, jotting down prices. Other than that, however, the project was quite enjoyable.

We learned a lot from this project. We not only learned which store consistently had the cheapest overall prices, but later when we moved I did price surveys on grocery stores in the new area to find out where I should do my shopping. I'm sure I never would have done this if it hadn't been for the research project. You have to be alert to changes in a program of this type and do a survey every so often to see if the same store is still maintaining its low prices.

My mother had always been a bargain hunter, so I'd had a good example set for me. She always read the weekly grocery ads to see which store had better buys. However, my husband warned me that I mustn't save money on groceries and spend it on gas driving to several stores.

During the first years of our marriage when our food storage was somewhat limited, I made out weekly menus according to what was on sale each week. Later, when I could rely more on my stock on hand, I bought more case lots of items that were on special, and arranged our menus more around what we had on hand. I soon learned what kinds of things I used all the time and needed to have in quantities. Anything I was short of was put on a list to buy for that week along with fresh items. We did a lot of canning and freezing of vegetables and fruits. We also dried a lot of fruit and vegetables. Sources of good produce at reasonable prices have to be available to make this worthwhile. We have had a dehydrator for the past few years and so can take advantage of many more bargains.

My sister's father-in-law taught me a great lesson about shopping. He was financially well-off but still looked for bargains. He told me about a discount store where I could get railroad-damaged and surplus groceries that were still of good quality. I shopped there and found many bargains. Because he alerted me to the fact that there are always special deals to be had, I have done a little more searching. One has to be up on one's knowledge of prices, however, or the so-called bargains may not be the bargain they seem. When I find a good price on an item that I will use (or else it's not a bargain), I buy just as much of that item as I can afford.

My husband is excellent at budgeting, so I don't have to worry about that part of the finances. But I have become, through practice, a better shopper for groceries. The first month I was in bed before the triplets were born, Gerald bought all the groceries. At the end of the month when he tallied up our budget, he discovered he had spent almost twice as much on groceries as I ever had. After that he came in with the newspapers and asked me to make out a grocery list for him.

Another thing I have always done is to mentally tabulate the amount I'm spending as I put items in the grocery cart. In the first few years of marriage I did this out of necessity, so I wouldn't spend more money than I had. In more recent years, it's mainly because I want to know how much I'm spending. I don't want to be shocked at the checkout stand. Besides, my husband is strict on budgeting, and I have to stay within the limits he sets.

One homemaking day in Relief Society we had a lesson on organizing and scheduled planning in our homes. As the teacher was concluding her lesson she said, "Janice, will you share some of your secrets with us? You always seem to accomplish so much." I told her she really didn't want me to comment, but she insisted. I totally undid her lesson with my comments, which she couldn't have foreseen.

She had taught us to plan our menus out weekly and even monthly. Also, the lesson said that our work schedule should be planned out on a daily, weekly, monthly, and yearly schedule. I told the class that in my earlier years of marriage I had lived on a strict schedule both with menus and housework, and had found out I couldn't accomplish nearly as much that way. For instance, if my schedule said today was the day I had planned to clean my ovens and refrigerator, and I just wasn't in the mood for that kind of cleaning, it could take me twice as long to do the job. Or if I had planned on my menu to make homemade noodles, and I really didn't feel like it, it became a chore instead of fun. I learned I could accomplish a lot more if I weren't tied to a day-to-day or week-to-week plan. Some days I'd get up and really feel in the mood to clean. I could accomplish about five times as much by doing it when I felt like it. I realize a woman has to be careful when using unorthodox planning or she could accomplish nothing. Remember, we get where we're heading, even if that's nowhere. Maybe it wouldn't work for too many people, but it has worked much better for me.

I can awaken in the morning and feel like baking. I can spend the greater part of the day baking, after doing the necessities, and really put out a lot. I may make six large loaves of white bread, seven large loaves of wheat bread, four loaves of French bread, a double batch of hard rolls, eight dozen cinnamon rolls, twisties, Danish pastries, and sweet rolls. Sure, I'm tired at the end of the day, but I've enjoyed it and it hasn't seemed like work. Now if I were to do all that when I didn't feel like it, I'd be defeated before I started.

I've made five dresses in one day when I really felt like sewing. Other times when I really didn't feel like sewing—which isn't very often—I've done nothing but spoil one article. I've become a real proponent of doing what I feel like doing, unless it interferes with the smooth running of my household.

Of course, there are things that always have to be done. Some can be done on a very relaxed schedule and others can't. For instance, canning has to be done pretty much when the food is available. We may have a choice of a few days, but the timing is essentially fixed. Spring cleaning and fall cleaning, on the other hand, can be done during a several-week span. I have done my spring cleaning as late as June and fall cleaning as late as December. Who says it has to be done at a certain time of the year? We need to make our own rules and stop caring what others think.

It helps to know in my mind, or even write them down, what things have to be done in my home. Then I set a time span when I'd like them accomplished—maybe one to three months or one to two weeks. Then I can do them when I feel most inclined. There are things that have to be done daily whether I feel like it or not, except in rare emergencies. I have found that I'm much happier if I do these jobs as quickly as I can. For instance, now that all my children are in school, I try to have breakfast dishes washed, kitchen cleaned, vacuuming finished, house straightened, exercising done, scriptures read, and prayers said by 9 A.M. That way I have the rest of the day to accomplish all the other things I need to do and want to do. My husband says I set impossible goals and then set about trying to achieve them.

As I've said, my methods are unorthodox and probably wouldn't work for all people. I'm not lazy, and I'm not afraid of a lot of work. I don't sit around and do nothing either: there are too many exciting things in life that I want to learn about and to learn how to do for me to waste time. I have been able to fulfill these desires more because of my unorthodox planning. If a woman doesn't work well without a scheduled routine and a scheduled menu, then by all means she should use one. I used one completely the first few years of marriage, but I felt tied down and unhappy working that way. I'm much more relaxed, much happier, and I accomplish much more by planning more according to my moods. I still plan. It's just that my planning for one day may be done the morning of that day or the evening before.

After reading this some people may say, "If I worked that way, I'd be running to the store for every meal I fixed." Then this system probably wouldn't work for them. I have learned to shop in such a way that I have on hand things I need for the types of meals I prepare. Sometimes if I'm asked to make a special dish for some occasion I may lack an ingredient or two, but that's the exception and not the rule. I make a note of things when I'm running short so I can replace these items—at a sale price, if possible.

Whatever system a woman uses, she shouldn't let homemaking become a drudge. If we hate housework, it's because we choose to hate it—we always have another choice. So we might as well make up our minds to be good mothers and housewives and enjoy what we do. We'll be much happier, and so will everyone else. And the bonus feature is that we'll accomplish much more.

If I really have a need to accomplish a lot on certain days, I get up before the children do. I can accomplish so much more when I'm not interrupted and I'm fresh. If my children begin awakening at 6 A.M., I get up at 4 A.M. If I'm going to be arising at this hour for an extended time, I feel much better if I go to bed in the evening right after the children do. This way I can still get an adequate amount of sleep and have the extra two free hours that will enable me to accomplish much more. These two hours early in the morning were my sewing hours when my children were tiny. On one or two occasions I have even stayed up all night when I had deadlines to meet. I don't recommend it as a general practice because it's not healthy, but it won't kill anyone to go without one or two nights' sleep in a lifetime.

One thing I have never done is to go back to bed once I'm up. I heard one lady say she always made her bed as soon as she climbed out of it so she wouldn't be tempted to climb back in. I've never had that problem. Sometimes I have wished I didn't have to get up when the alarm went off, but once I am up I have no great desire to return to bed. I heard another lady say that since she hated to get up she'd never go back to bed because then she'd have to do it twice in one day.

I have also learned to operate at one speed—fast. Anything I'm doing I try to finish as quickly as possible. If I'm putting things away in different rooms or going to different areas of the house, I run. It's not only faster, but I get a little more exercise that way. When we lived in houses with basements, I ran up and down the stairs too.

I'm always on the lookout for quicker and easier methods of doing things. Sometimes I find I'm further ahead spending a little time meditating on different methods of accomplishing a task rather than just diving right in and doing it the most obvious way. When I'm away from home, I make a mental note of how other people do things. We can always learn from others.

I remember my older sister saying that someone had teased her because every time she did the dishes she took a few minutes and wiped off all the cabinets. To me, it's much easier to do that with each batch of dishes than to let it become a big weekly task. I noticed once when I visited this same sister that she not only wiped off the cabinets but she washed around the back doorknob—inside and out. With so many children going in and out our house each day, I decided this was a good idea for me to copy. I also washed off the wall around the dinner table. I'm sure every little hand in our house passed over that wall to and from the table despite the many times the children were reminded.

Little hints such as these that we pick up from others can make our overall household tasks much simpler. By cutting down on the amount of time spent in cleaning the house, we have more time to teach and work with our children and more time to spend developing talents in other areas.

Chapter 8

Cheaper by the Dozen?

The old saying that things are cheaper by the dozen doesn't refer to having children. But the blessings of a large family far outweigh the expenses. I have come to know in a very real way that God does know all things and "there is not anything save he knows it." (2 Nephi 9:20.) By tapping this vast source of knowledge, we can learn to do many things for ourselves. Many things we would ordinarily hire other people to do can be done by us if we tap this source of knowledge. I have learned that God truly knows how to make drapes, upholster, tailor a man's suit, carpenter, and even fix things around the house.

By being a little self-reliant and doing a lot of reading and studying and watching of other people, I have been able to learn a great deal about how to do many things. When I have progressed to the stage where my learning needs a little expert polishing, then I seek out the Lord's help. He has never failed me. When the answers have come, they have always been so simple I have wondered why I didn't think of them on my own.

When Beckie was born, hospital and doctor bills weren't nearly as high as they are today, but neither was our income. I hadn't been able to work for two months before she was born. My husband was in his third year of college and had a part-time job. He was making about $135 (take-home pay) per month. My parents had helped us buy a home so our rent money would be going toward something, and our house payment was $90 a month—$15 more than our rent had been. Out of the remaining money we had to pay tithing, ward budget, and utilities; buy groceries and gas for the car (we rode the bus as often as possible because it was cheaper); save for tuition for Gerald's schooling; and save for a baby. Logically, there was no way we could have done it, but somehow we did. I had always been taught that having a family was what the Lord expected us to do, and that if we kept the law, the Lord would bless us.

Beckie arrived well and very healthy and without complications. I was also blessed with an abundance of milk, so I could nurse her and didn't have to buy formula for her. She ate well and had no physical problems. I took her back for her six-week checkup and she didn't go to the doctor again till she had her tonsils out. My sister took me with her to the county health department to get the shots Beckie needed (as recommended by the doctor).

By the time Debbie and Eric arrived, Gerald had been out of school for five months. Paying for their birth was somewhat easier, although the doctor charged extra for delivering multiple births, and, of course, the hospital expense was higher. They were born five weeks early, so they needed to be in incubators at first. Their stay in the hospital was also longer than Beckie's. In spite of the increased costs, it still seemed easier to pay for their birth expenses than it had been for Beckie's.

Two years later, when Kerry and Kyle were born, Gerald had started a new job with new insurance. However, insurance companies almost never pay for pregnancies that occur before the policy is taken out, and I was already pregnant when Gerald started the job. Our finances were limited, and we knew it would be very difficult to pay for another baby at that time. However, we were keeping the commandment by having our family, and the Lord blessed us again. The insurance paid for Kerry and Kyle's birth expenses.

When I was pregnant so soon again after Kerry and Kyle were born, we weren't worried about the expenses because we knew we were covered by insurance. However, when we found out it would probably be a multiple birth again (I thought there were more than two from the first time I felt life), we became somewhat concerned because we would have to pay most of the extra hospital expenses.

The Lord was watching out for us again, though. We couldn't possibly have known what great expenses we were about to incur, but the Lord knew. One month before the triplets were born, Gerald's insurance was changed. The major change occurred in the maternity benefits, and this made it possible for us to leave the hospital having paid a total of ten cents for a phone call I'd made. Without the change in the insurance, we would have had to pay for incubators, special equipment, special care, medicines, and other incidentals required to take care of three two-month premature babies for three weeks. It would have been a heavy burden for us for a long time.

After all those multiple births, it seemed easy to pay for our last child, a single, beautiful baby girl.

Somehow with each new birth we had been able to manage our finances to pay for the increased needs. When the triplets came, the doctor made me dry up in the hospital when he found out how long the triplets would have to stay there. He felt it would be too hard to keep myself milked out for that length of time. As a result we were going to need a lot of formula.

My mother, unbeknown to me, called Dr. Snow and asked him if there weren't some way we could get a reduced price on formula. He talked to the route man who gave us two free cases but no reduced price. I was grateful and mortified at the same time.

The Lord had always blessed us in the past, and I felt certain he would again. Gerald and I had learned to struggle when he was still in college, when all we had to eat some days were some canned peaches my sister had given us. She had peach trees and wanted to put fresh fruit in her bottles that summer, so she gave us some extra to help her use them up. I don't think she ever knew how much we needed them and how grateful we were to have them. When the first twins were small, another sister's husband worked on a farm. Many times she brought us surplus milk, and I could buy cracked eggs there for fifteen cents a dozen. The Lord always seemed to guide us and bless us so that we never went without.

The summer before the triplets were born, I was very concerned about my canning. I wanted to have enough fruit canned so I could make my own baby food and still have plenty for my other children. My brother came over and told me he could get me some peaches for one dollar a bushel. He would bring me as many as I wanted. I talked it over with Gerald, and we decided to buy ten bushels. The problem was getting them canned, as I was confined to bed. Gerald brought a chaise lounge into the kitchen, and I lay on that and helped peel peaches. My mother came over in the evenings and helped us too. Somehow with three of us working, we managed to get all the peaches put up. Our bottles were scarce, so we crammed as many peaches into a bottle as we could.

Though my bottles were all full, I still wanted to can some pears, applesauce, and grapes. We figured out our finances and decided we could afford to buy the fruit. However, we simply couldn't afford to buy more bottles. We thought of everything we could do and still we couldn't come up with a solution. The fruit was cheaper than the bottles, and even if we bought a few bottles, we wouldn't be able to fit much fruit into them.

While I was in this quandary and feeling quite desperate about having enough fruit, I went to the Lord and told him our plight. I felt quite certain we were having more than two babies this time. I knew how much food it would take to feed all my small children. Fruit was cheap and plentiful that year; perhaps the next year it would be expensive and scarce. All these things were on my mind as I talked with the Lord.

After dinner that evening the phone rang. It was the bishop. He said he and his wife had been cleaning out their garage. They had about two hundred extra canning jars and wondered if I could use them.

I was so emotional with humble thanksgiving to the Lord that I could hardly answer him. The Lord had heard my prayers and was blessing us again! How unworthy I felt, but ever so grateful. That he was so aware of me and my problem was indeed humbling.

Many times the Lord interceded in our behalf. One year some friends inherited some land and built a lovely new home. On the land were several apricot trees. We loved nectar and also dried a lot of apricots and apricot leather. That particular year, apricots were scarce and expensive. We couldn't afford very many. We had canned two bushels when these friends called and told us to come and help them use their apricots. We were elated! While we were there, they told us to help ourselves to some grapes as well.

People always seemed to be on the lookout for us. We'd get a call from a friend or a neighbor telling us where there were raspberries we could pick, or where there were assorted berries available at a good price, or where we could get good pickling cucumbers at a reasonable rate.

During the early years of our marriage the Lord had blessed me with the ability to stretch our meager food budget so we had sufficient to eat. I particularly remember how I learned to make one chicken last several days. I would buy a large stewing hen when hens were on sale for nineteen cents a pound. I'd cook it on Monday, covering it with water and adding chopped onions, celery, leaves, and half a grated carrot for flavor. When the chicken was nearly done, I'd remove it from the stock and allow it to dry somewhat and cool. Then I'd cover it and put it in the refrigerator. I made noodles to go in the broth and we ate that on Monday with enough left over for some lunches during the week. On Tuesday I'd baste the outside of the chicken with melted butter, make dressing from dried bread, and stuff the chicken and bake it along with some potatoes. I'd save enough chicken meat from Tuesday's meal to make a chicken gravy like my mother made: using leftover chicken, add a chopped onion and barely cover with water. Bring to a boil and simmer a few minutes till the onions are tender. Add canned milk (as much as water previously added) and more regular milk to make the amount of gravy you want. Heat that through and thicken. Add a can of cream of chicken soup and mix thoroughly. Serve over potatoes or rice or add some frozen peas to gravy and serve over patty shells. This can also be used as a filling for chicken pie by adding cooked potato and carrot cubes and peas and baking it in unbaked pie shells. In this manner I could serve my family a variety of meals and still use only one chicken that cost about seventy-five cents.

In clothing our family, again we were blessed. I had two older sisters who passed baby clothes back and forth. When we started having our family, they shared the clothes with me too. They also spent time teaching me how to do the special embroidery they put on the baby clothes.

We always seemed to have neighbors with children just a little bit older than ours, and they always shared their hand-me-downs. I really don't know how we would have managed without their help. My time was so limited that I didn't always have time to sew, so we used many of the hand-me-downs just as they were. There were also many that I altered to fit the styles and the children better. Some of the clothes the triplets wore had been handed down and worn by five other girls before they got to them. They had been taken care of so well that many of them were still almost like new.

Sewing was one of my favorite pastimes. It became a challenge to see something in a store that cost nearly twenty-five dollars and go home and make it for less than two. My sister gave me the initial encouragement. When I'd see something that I really liked but couldn't afford, she'd tell me I could make it. I watched material sales and bought fabric only when it was available for a really good price.

As more children arrived in our family, my sewing time seemed to be more limited, and at the same time it became more necessary. For some period when my children were small, the only time I could find for sewing was early in the morning. By getting up at 4 A.M. I could work for two hours without interruption. I tried to have my articles cut out so that this was strictly sewing time. I made most of the children's clothing, including all their underwear as well as their T-shirts, coats, and suits. I had found that the budget fabric department of a local store carried many factory leftovers, and I could purchase knit fabrics there that weren't available in the regular stores. I also recycled many clothes, such as making my sons' suits from suits that were given to me. When people heard I did this, suits came to me from many sources. At one time I had three large boxes of men's suits in my basement, only one of which came from family members. I used buttons and zippers off the suits so all I had to buy was thread. I also made coats for the children from old coats given me. I made my own coats and clothes and my husband's shirts, pants, and suits. From my mother-in-law, I learned to take apart wool coats and make rugs that were practically indestructible. I wasted very little, and the Lord blessed me with knowledge and the ability to make the time available so that I could sew for my family.

We'd had quite a struggle initially when we moved into our first home. My folks had given us the down payment, and we had no furniture of our own to put into it. My parents gave us an old couch and chair, a card table, and a couple of stools. My brother donated an old bed he wasn't using. That was the extent of our furniture. For a chest of drawers, I obtained some orange crates and fastened them together, then padded the top and covered it with oilcloth. A drawstring cover, made from old curtains, completed the effect.

There was no overhead light in our living room, and we didn't have a lamp to put in there. It was embarrassing not to be able to turn on a light for visitors. My sister took a wrought-iron tripod and attached an old lamp socket to it with a plug so we'd have a light for the living room.

I remember well the first lamp we bought. We had been so extremely frugal for so long that it seemed like a real extravagance to even think about buying a lamp, but a department store was having a sale, so we decided we'd look anyway. We looked at every lamp they had marked down. Finally we found one we thought we could afford. It cost $10, and I thought it was the most beautiful lamp in all the world. After we set it up in the living room, I kept going in just to admire it. We didn't buy living room furniture until we had been married twelve years, but even when we did, I don't think anything ever meant as much to me as that first lamp.

When Gerald graduated from college and started working full time, things were somewhat easier for a while. Then we started increasing our family by twos and threes and our expenses also shot up. Gerald had always been excellent at managing money, and he decided that if we didn't start saving while things were difficult, we'd never reach a point where things were easy enough so we could save. He started putting a little money away each payday.

After the triplets arrived, we were in desperate need of a larger house. Our bishop and the elders in our ward were willing to add onto the house for us if we would buy the materials. We were living in a small, two-bedroom place, and Gerald decided it just wasn't practical to add on, so we started house hunting. We did a lot of looking, a lot of thinking, and a lot of praying, and finally decided we could get more for our money if we built a house. When we went to settle the financial details, we found out there would have been no way we could have built our house without our savings. How grateful I was for a husband who had foresight enough to save even in hard times.

Another thing that Gerald always did was to pay cash for purchases. And he found out some stores would give ninety days credit without charging interest, so we could establish a credit rating and still have a leverage with the company in case of faulty merchandise.

Gerald was a real bargain hunter and was always asking for a discount. One time we went to a sale of fire-damaged goods to buy a mattress. When we made our selection, Gerald asked how much discount he could get for paying cash. The salesman told him nothing. He asked if the store would carry the purchase for ninety days with no interest or the same as cash. The salesman said they would. Gerald then proceeded to point out all the bookkeeping time they'd save if he paid cash. The salesman agreed but still said he couldn't reduce the price for cash. So Gerald asked to see the manager. At this point I left the store, totally embarrassed. After talking to the manager, Gerald not only received a reduction in price, but the manager offered him a job. He couldn't understand why I was embarrassed. The sale price on the mattress was sixteen dollars, and he finally bought it for fifteen dollars cash.

When we moved into the new house we had built, it was little more than a shell. The basement wasn't finished, and our three boys were sleeping down there. My father had given us some used lumber, which we used to build shelves for our storage room. Every month we tried to buy something for the house. It was quite a struggle, but eventually we were able to get the boys' room somewhat roughed in.

I made drapes for every room except the living room. I worked at it quite diligently, and I learned a lot. However, I didn't feel confident enough to make the living room drapes. My new neighbor had had some made for her home, and I really liked the way they were done. Gerald and I discussed it, and he finally agreed to let me have ours made professionally. I was really excited, for we had lived in the house a year and still didn't have drapes in the living room. I made my selection for sheers and a heavy damask over-drape that went wall-to-wall. When the saleslady figured it all up, the price came to $300. I could tell that Gerald wasn't very happy about it, but we went ahead and bought them. When they arrived and were hung, I examined them thoroughly. I decided that there simply couldn't be that much to making drapes and having them look so nice, and I vowed I'd never pay that much money for drapes again.

Some new people moved into our ward, and I was assigned there as a visiting teacher. After a few months, I discovered the wife made her own draperies. They looked really nice, so I began quizzing her about them. She gave me a set of instructions, prepared by a local college, for making drapes. She told me where she bought her drapery fabric, and I started watching the newspaper for a sale. When I finally found one, we went to the shop and my neighbor helped me select fabric for some new kitchen drapes. That set turned out much more professional looking than my others. I had done a lot of looking at my living room drapes to see how the professionals did theirs. I had also read everything I could about making draperies. I watched for another sale and when one came, I bought fabric to make drapes for my bedroom. I tried a more difficult set this time: a series of three tie-backs with sheers underneath. I studied it out well in my mind before I began the project. Again, the finished drapes were quite professional looking.

There was one thing that stumped me for a while. The folds in professionally made draperies always looked a little better than homemade ones. In fact, that was the main thing that made homemade drapes look homemade. I thought and thought and just didn't seem to be able to come up with a method that would give the professional look. I had about decided it was something that only came with a lot of practice and was ready to give up in despair. Finally, however, I presented my problem to the Lord. He answered my prayer, and the method that came to my mind was so simple, I wondered how I had failed to figure it out for myself.

I had previously sewn in the pocket for the three tiny pleats and immediately creased the pocket into the three tiny pleats and tacked them in place. The method I felt inspired to use was to sew in all the pockets for the pleats and then put the folds into the drapery and tie it in several places along the length. This process of folding required two people with two steel tapes or wooden yardsticks—one person at the top of the drapery and one at the bottom. The person at the top measured from pleat pocket to pleat pocket and gave the measurement to the person at the bottom. She then measured off the same distance and marked it with a pin. After all the measuring was done, both would pick the drapery up at the measured spot and lay it on top of another fold. This was repeated till all of the drape was folded. Then the drapery was tied about six times down the length to hold the folds in place, and set aside for a week. At the end of the waiting period, the top of the drapery was untied, and the three tiny pleats were finger-pressed in and machine tacked. The top of the drapery was then retied for at least another day.

A few years later I had occasion to speak to a professional drapery maker. When she found out about my experience, she wanted to know the details of my folding method. I was hesitant to tell her, thinking perhaps my method was stupid, but she kept pressing me. When I finally explained, she told me that was how the professionals did it.

After reflecting on this experience a great deal, I discovered that God truly does know all things, and what we can learn is limitless if we only put ourselves in tune so we can tap this source of knowledge.

From making draperies I branched out and started doing other window treatments. My niece knew of a window shade factory that would sell fabric to the public, so I decided to make some shades. The ones I tried to put wallpaper on just didn't work too well. They were much too heavy to roll. Others with lighter weight covering worked fine. I found I could buy regular fabric and dip it in a special solution to make it as sturdy as shade fabric. I found different types of backing that I could iron on or glue on to regular fabric. I have even used upholstery fabric alone to make shades.

Once each year Gerald used to take me to a home show where I—with notebook in hand—got many ideas for window treatment and home decorating. Model homes are always a good place to see in real life a variety of decorating and window treatment techniques.

Learning how to upholster was my next goal. We had finally invested in some living room furniture, which Gerald told me would have to last fifteen years. He thought it was expensive, but I had done a lot of looking and it was not overpriced. Still, I thought I could save money if I could do my own upholstering. I finally persuaded Gerald into taking an upholstery class with me through a high school adult education program. After that class I felt confident I could do other things on my own. I feel sincerely that the Lord has helped me and guided me in being able to learn to accomplish many things as a wife, mother, and homemaker.

Over the years, many people asked me to sew for them. I usually did only weddings, however. I made many, many wedding dresses and bridesmaid's dresses. Once it took me seventy hours just to glue the lace on a dress with a toothpick. I was copying a very exclusive and expensive gown.

When my husband and I arrived at the reception center, the owner told me she had never seen such a beautiful dress. She asked if she could refer brides-to-be to me to have their wedding dresses made. I thanked her but declined, because I didn't even have time to do all the ones I was presently being asked to do. I marveled at how I was able to make such items, and at the confidence I had that I could do it. But I prayed about each garment I made, and the Lord obviously was listening and helping me.

Home economics hadn't been my major in college, but I was certainly getting a practical education in it. I was always being inspired with easier ways to do things and better shortcuts. I also read a lot, knowing it always helps to get other people's ideas. One summer some people in our ward opened a fabric shop and asked if I'd teach sewing classes there. I had taught some classes in my home because several friends had requested it. Teaching professionally was a little more frightening, but I finally decided to do it. I taught several classes during the summer evenings when my husband was home with the children. I didn't enjoy being away from home, however, and was glad when the shop was sold and the classes were discontinued.

That fall my neighbor went to work, and I agreed to tend her two children. From the money I earned we were able to finish most of the basement, and I learned how to do a little carpentering. Our bishop's wife had done most of the work in her basement, and this gave me the courage to try. I did some paneling, some Perfotaping, and some general carpentry. Gerald was elders quorum president, and he had very little time to help out. I was too impatient to wait till he could do it, so I tackled many things myself that I probably otherwise wouldn't have done.

I learned a great lesson in buying carpet. We shopped several places and finally thought we had found a good bargain. A man came out from the store and measured the basement and gave us an estimate. A man in our ward was a partner in a carpet shop, and somehow we felt impressed to look at what he had also. We found a piece we liked, but it was more per yard than the other carpet had been. However, we finally decided to have him come and measure. When he was finished I was very impressed.

The first man had measured and figured the total square feet, and then had used a chart to estimate the yardage. The man from our ward, on the other hand, drew a shape of the room and put the measurements on the drawing. Then he drew a shape of the carpet with measurements and figured exactly how he would have to cut it to fit the shape of the room. When he completed the figuring, he quoted fifteen yards less than the first man. I asked him if he were sure. He was. He said he always figured it out that way so he wouldn't waste carpet, and the buyers didn't have big pieces left over for which they had had to pay. It was a little more work, but it saved a good deal of money.

Our large family was quite hard on kitchen tables and

chairs. We had purchased a kitchen set before we moved to our new home, but our children seemed to be able to demolish vinyl-covered chairs in no time at all. We found some plastic-molded chairs at a bargain price and bought twelve of them, but the chairs had a rough finish and we found them very difficult to keep clean. Our table wasn't large enough when the triplets outgrew the highchair stage, so my father came and took the table apart, inserted a four-foot piece of plywood in the middle, and covered it with Formica. He built a wooden support leg underneath it. We now had a large enough table for all of us to sit down at once. It lasted for several years, and then the chairs began breaking apart from the legs.

We knew we had to buy a new set, so we started saving and looking. We were aghast at the prices. A table and chair set large enough for our family would have cost over $300, and all the sets had the vinyl-covered chairs that I knew wouldn't last too long. I was quite discouraged. Then I remembered having seen an ad in the paper for a shop that would custom-make wood furniture. We decided to drive out and look at what they had. They had a big catalog of early American furniture styles they would make. We looked a long time at the trestle table and benches. I kept thinking how nice it would be not to have to move eleven chairs every time I was vacuuming. The manager took us out into his shop and showed us some trestle tables being built. The workmanship looked excellent. When we still hesitated, he suggested we go to a shop carrying similar furniture and examine their products. So we did.

We liked what we saw, but Gerald makes it a policy to sleep on every decision before making a purchase. We slept on it and decided to have a trestle table made. We ordered a seven by four-foot table with two benches, two armless ladder-back chairs, and one ladder-back with arms. The total cost was less than a kitchen set with vinyl chairs would have been. It proved to be a very good purchase. We have been using the set for over eight years, and there is only slight wear on the caning on one chair.

I know the Lord has blessed us in making wise decisions financially. We have made some poor ones from which we learned great lessons, but generally we have been blessed. We have also been blessed to learn how to do things ourselves at much less cost.

The marvelous thing about learning to do all these things

was that from the money saved I could afford piano lessons for my children. Music has always been important in my life, and I wanted my children to gain at least a little appreciation for music.

My sister lived near us when my older children were old enough to take lessons. She was an excellent pianist and also very good with children. Besides, she was willing to work out a program with me where I could do sewing for her in partial payment for the lessons. As the children grew she taught more of them; the older five were all taking lessons from her at one time. It was quite a challenge to organize so each one had adequate time to practice each day.

When it no longer was practical, because of conflicting schedules, to have my sister teach the children, the Lord seemed to open up another door. I was able to persuade a dear friend who was very talented musically to teach some of us. She didn't ordinarily enjoy teaching but she was willing to try. The children really learned to love and appreciate her. When we moved to Phoenix, one of their great woes was "We'll never find another teacher like Sister Winters."

For a while it seemed that was true. Then one day an acquaintance called me on the phone. She was one of the most talented musicians in the valley. She told me she had decided to start teaching piano again but was going to take only a few students. For some reason, she said, my name had been on her mind all day. She asked if I had any children who would be interested in taking piano lessons. Did I! I had three. I wondered at the blessing that was coming from the Lord again. Emmy was not only willing to take the three children, but also insisted on giving me a special rate because I would have so many taking lessons.

It has been my experience that when we're earnestly trying, the Lord is always there to help us. Many doors have been opened to us, and the blessings have come flooding in. It always makes me feel so weak and humble when I "count my many blessings."

Another program that I'm sure we were inspired to begin when the children were little was a savings program for them. One of our neighbors told his older boys that when they earned money, they could either put 25 percent of it in a savings account or pay that amount to the parents for board and room. Gerald and I thought this an excellent idea. We decided to vary it a little and start with the children right then. Beckie was about five, Debbie and Eric, three, and Kerry and Kyle, one. We told them that when they earned money, we expected them to put half of it into a savings account for missions and college. Otherwise they could pay it to us for board and room. Of course, they were too little at the time to understand much about it. We opened an account for each one, and the bank gave them each a coin bank in which to put their money. When I was sewing for a dress shop, I paid the children each time I got paid, somewhat like an allowance. Out of this they put their tithing in one container, their savings in the coin bank, and their spendings in another container. This really was a valuable learning experience for them. It not only taught them to pay tithing and how to save, but also kept the idea of college and missions on their minds.

From their meager spendings, they soon learned to budget their money so they'd have some to spend on each other at Christmastime. We had always spent time together during the Christmas season making presents for one another that didn't cost much. As they learned to budget their money, however, the children could make bigger and better items or tuck in a little purchased goodie along with the items they had made. The children became quite ingenious at making gifts that cost little or nothing. One of the older girls helped one of the triplets make a coupon book for each of her brothers. The coupons were for making beds, dusting, doing dishes, and other chores they had. The boys really enjoyed these coupon books, and were a little saddened when their sister grew older and had a little more money and no longer wished to give them a coupon book. I think most of the excitement at Christmas, when the children were little, came as a result of all the time and effort they put into making gifts for each other.

Both Gerald and I had worked our way through college. We had seen many students who were being fully supported by their parents, and who often seemed to be content with doing mediocre work and just having pleasure from their time at school. Some of them really didn't seem to appreciate what they had or the sacrifices their parents were making for them. We were both determined that our children would do all they could on their own. We'd be willing to help them if they needed help, but they must first do all they could on their own. We felt sure they'd not only appreciate it more, but would also be willing to work harder if they were spending their own money. Because of this, our girls were encouraged to babysit as soon as they were old enough. When the boys reached twelve, they were encouraged to get paper routes. Having a paper boy in the family is not the easiest thing, and having three is even harder. You're really tied to home much the same as if you had a cow. However, we felt it would be worth it. The boys were learning to work, to be dependable, and to handle their own money, and were able to help pay for their own needs. In a measure they were learning to become independent.

It's strange how different children can be when they've had essentially the same training. Eric turned out to be more frugal than his dad in some ways. He kept records of his money, and had a chart showing his income and where all of it went. Most of the extra went into savings. He splurged occasionally on coins for his collection. One day he came home from a trip to the shopping mall with a bag, and I wondered what had been his big splurge. He opened the sack and displayed his purchase—a book on the life of Albert Einstein. Not the usual splurge most fifteen-year-old boys would make. He was always careful with his money and anything else he had. He worked hard in school, hoping for a scholarship to help pay his college expenses.

When Eric was a junior in high school, he made a trip to Provo, Utah, and applied for early admission and a scholarship to Brigham Young University. He received both. He worked hard the summer before going to college. He wanted to earn as much money as he could toward his mission, since he couldn't take extra time away from school and still retain his scholarship. He found a job working at a plastics factory; the only problem was that it was seventeen miles from home. He rode his bike seventeen miles twice a day in the scorching Phoenix summer heat to earn money. At school he didn't want to touch the money he had saved for his mission, so he found a job and worked while trying to maintain a 3.5 grade average in order to retain his scholarship.

The girls have also been blessed in finding work. They haven't had jobs handed to them—they've had to go out and find their own. Sometimes this was quite discouraging. Eventually, when they did find jobs, they weren't always ones they really enjoyed. Beckie always felt that attitude was the important thing. She'd go and look and look, and when she had nowhere else to turn she'd say, "Well, I've done all I can do and now the Lord will bless me." And he always does. Some of her jobs have been very tedious—such as looking through a microscope all day making stereo needles. She'd come home tired from sitting in such a cramped position all day, but grateful to have a job and happy.

"The Lord helps those who help themselves." Our children have found this to be a true statement, and have learned to use their own initiative and then depend on the Lord for help.

Chapter 9

Cruisin' for a Bruisin'

Numerous books have been written on discipline. Many church lessons have been devoted to the subject. My first real introduction to different methods of disciplining was in a child growth and development class at Brigham Young University. It helped me set many goals that proved to be of much value after I was married and had children of my own.

One of the things I have learned over the years is that there is a definite difference between disciplining and punishing. A simple way to differentiate is to say that disciplining is the Lord's way and punishing is Satan's way. Discipline is an effective long-term method of control, while punishment is an emotional short-term method of control. Of course, discipline is much more effective.

As I have studied the scriptures, the Lord's way seems to be to establish laws. If you live the law you receive the blessing; if you break the law, you must suffer the consequences. For example, the Lord told Adam and Eve in the Garden of Eden not to partake of the forbidden fruit. They were told the consequences for breaking the law. Well, they chose to break the law and had to suffer the consequences. The Lord didn't yell and scream and fly in a rage at them. He merely told them what would be the consequences of their actions.

When I was first married, I was determined I would never spank my children, but would teach them the proper way, with love. Beckie's personality fit right in with my plans. If I ever even said no to her, it seemed to break her heart. To our dismay, most of the other children didn't come equipped with that type of personality.

We learned, through trial and error, methods that were more effective for us. Some of the methods I tried were recommended to me by others. Some I wish I had never tried—they were too severe and certainly not in keeping with my earlier resolves.

I shall never forget the day I lost control and punished my eldest son in anger. My nerves were very bad during the second year with our first set of twins. I think I was worn down mentally and physically, but that still was no excuse. I don't remember what my son had done (he was about two), but I remember grabbing him and flinging him against the wall. Immediately I regretted my loss of temper. I rushed over and picked him up and was greatly relieved to find that he wasn't injured. I knelt down right then and thanked the Lord for protecting him, and vowed I would never punish again in anger. And I never have. When I am the angriest I just leave the scene without saying anything.

Deciding upon an effective method of discipline for small children was very difficult for me. I always tried to put as much of the responsibility on the child as I could. The Lord had given Adam his choice, and I wanted to do the same with my children. This is how it worked: after I had given a specific direction to a child, I began slowly counting to ten. If the child chose to obey before I reached ten, everything was fine. If the child didn't obey by the time I reached ten, he or she received a couple of swats on the bottom—only a couple and always on the bottom.

To begin this program with each child, I explained to him before I started counting that I was going to count to ten. If he did as he had been told, everything would be fine, but if he didn't obey, then I would have to spank him. It didn't take long till the children really understood what it meant when I started counting.

When they were about three years old, two of my children were quite defiant when I began counting. They weren't about to do as they had been told. After a couple of swats on the bottom, I'd tell them I was going to count again. If they chose not to obey, they would get spanked again. This counting process was repeated about fifteen times before they finally obeyed. After that, I had no more problems with the children.

I was very careful to be consistent. Once I started counting, I followed through. If the child didn't obey, he got the spanking no matter where we were. Once we were returning home from a vacation in our station wagon. I was in front with my husband and the youngest children, and directly behind us were boxes full of groceries and camping supplies. Behind the boxes the rest of the kids were lying on the floor on sleeping bags. My oldest son was in the furthest corner from me when he began acting up. I started to count to ten, thinking that would solve the problem. He just ignored me, smirking, as he knew I couldn't reach him. When I reached ten and still he was disobedient, I put down the child I was holding, climbed up over the cooler and boxes, and crawled to the rear of the station wagon. I administered his swats and crawled back. He was in a state of shock, and so were the other children. Not one of them had thought I would follow through. But they didn't know I had been raised by a mother who believed being consistent was one of the Ten Commandments.

Another thing I was very consistent at doing was showing forth afterwards an increase of love toward him whom I had reproved, lest he esteem me to be his enemy. (See D&C 121:43.) We don't want our children to ever think we're upset with them personally—only with their actions. So I'd give them a few minutes to think about what they'd done, and then I'd sit down and take them on my lap and put my arms around them. I'd explain to them how much I loved them, and how it really hurt me inside (I'd point to my heart) when they were disobedient. I loved them and didn't want to have to spank them, but Heavenly Father had assigned me to be their mother, and I was responsible for them. If I didn't teach them the proper way to behave, Heavenly Father would not be pleased with me. I told them again that I loved them and hoped they'd remember next time what was the right thing to do.

This seemed to work so well that when I did have to discipline my children, they'd come and stand by me waiting to be reinstated and loved. Children need to have rules. They need to know what they can do and what they can't do. They're so much more secure if they know what's expected of them. Children will go just as far as you'll let them, but they're much happier when you set the limitations and stick to them.

I have seen how a child can get upset and have a tantrum when his mother refuses something, and then the mother changes her mind and gives in, thinking she's making her child happy. He's happy for a fleeting moment, but becomes a more cross and contentious child. I have had neighbor children in my home who would be completely content after I would explain our rules to them. When their mothers would come to get them, they would become totally different personalities—whiny and cross. They'd argue with their mothers, and the mothers seemed totally perplexed at how to handle the situation. Little children need a firmer hand. They grow to their independence, but it must be learned a step at a time. I firmly believe in giving children choices, but only the choices I decide upon, not the ones they select.

Parents should never argue with children. With little children, we need to quietly and respectfully insist they obey, but not beg them to do it. They soon learn to recognize the voice of authority and are much happier when they know they have to be obedient. When we plead with them to do something, they might decide not to, leaving us both cross. Arguing with children at any age merely invites the father of contention into our lives. There are much better ways of handling situations.

I have been asked many times if I believe in using rewards. Yes, I do. I've heard the comment that that's just another word for bribery, but I don't believe so—at least not the way I use them.

For example, my older five children were taking turns doing the evening dishes. Sometimes they took literally hours getting the dishes done, and as a result it became a job they disliked. When the situation got so bad I could no longer tolerate it, I knew I'd have to come up with an approach that would appeal to them and entice them into finishing their task more quickly. I told them how my younger sister and I had made doing dishes fun. We had divided up the tasks so we could work more efficiently. While one cleared the dishes from the table, the other put the food away. I usually washed and she dried. I'd separate the silverware into individual piles of knives, forks, spoons, and utensils so she could dry them and not have to sort them. We made a game of it by trying to beat the clock. We worked so well together that we could have the dishes completely finished—and to our mother's satisfaction—in less than five minutes. I tried to emphasize that we're always better off getting through a task quickly so we have time to do things more of our choosing.

To make the challenge I was giving the children more appealing, I offered a special treat each Saturday to the one who had done the dishes in the least time. If a child had an unusually large mess to clean up, we cut off a minute or two from his time. The challenge worked better than I ever dreamed it would. My oldest son was able to do the dishes for ten people in less than ten minutes, and he often got the reward. The dishes had to be done according to my lists, too. I inspected after the children were through, and if anything had to be redone, it was added to their time.

After a few months on this program, when the children realized how much more time was available to them if they did the job quickly, I removed the reward. They continued to work fast and effectively. They had really found it was to their advantage to do so.

Later, when the triplets and my youngest daughter were taking turns doing the dishes, this plan didn't seem to be as appealing. The triplets were older and more experienced and could easily have beaten their younger sister. When their dawdling annoyed me, I simply turned on the timer and told them to be finished before it went off. What would happen if they weren't finished in time, they wanted to know. I have always believed in using natural consequences as much as possible, so I simply told them they'd have to do the dishes the next night also.

Another natural consequence to use with older children is simply to explain to them the facts. They can work quickly and have a lot of free time, or they can work slowly and have no free time. It's up to them. A parent might work with them once to show how quickly the job can be done.

Sometimes when children dawdle and dislike their work, it may not mean they're lazy. My youngest daughter seemed to really hate doing dishes. I noticed, however, when we visited my mother, that this daughter was always one of the first in the kitchen to do the dishes. At first, I didn't pay too much attention to this because children always seem to enjoy working at someone else's house more than they do at their own.

One day she was helping me do the dishes at my mother's, and I noticed how happy she was. I started questioning her about it. How surprised I was at her answer. She loved doing the dishes at her grandmother's because she got to wash them by hand. (Grandmother didn't have a dishwasher.) I thought about that for a long time before the full impact of it hit me.

When we returned home I decided to test her out to see if I had surveyed the situation correctly. I talked to her the night it was her turn to do the dishes and told her she could wash them by hand if she'd rather. "Oh, goodie," she said. "Who's going to help me?" I told her she could wash and dry them by herself.

Her face clouded up, and she said in a sad voice, "But it won't be any fun then."

I had been right in my assumptions. It was loneliness that had brought on a distaste for the job. All the other children always had someone with whom to work, while she was alone. The other children were all closer together in age, about two years apart. But she was four years younger than the triplets.

As parents we have to be able to read between the lines, so to speak. We need to realize that what children say is not always at the root of a problem. Oftentimes they themselves aren't aware of what is actually wrong. We need guidance from above to help us see through situations such as these.

When disciplining children, it's most important that we don't use threats. It's one thing to establish rules and consequences; it's another thing to threaten a child. For instance, a mother may say to a child, "If you don't mind me, you're really going to get it when your father gets home." There are two things wrong with handling the situation in that way. First of all, mother is making father out to be the disciplinarian. Second, the child needs to be reprimanded while he's misbehaving. By the time dad's home, the child has usually long forgotten what he did wrong, and it's confusing for him to be disciplined when he is behaving.

A father usually has an easier time handling a child because he's not around so much, and the child is a little more fearful of his voice. However, a mother should never feel that she isn't capable of disciplining a child. I know the Lord will guide us if we ask for help in rearing our families. He is immensely interested in these little children. We just need to be more in tune so we will be blessed to handle difficult situations correctly. We can't just leave everything to the Lord, however—he expects us to learn for ourselves.

Each child should be well aware of the rules we have in our home and know that they will be enforced. Even then sometimes he may choose to disobey.

One day I went downstairs to my younger boys' room. I couldn't believe the sight that met my eyes. I got a large piece of newsprint and hung a big sign across the doorway: "No food for the inhabitants until this room is cleaned up!" I didn't say anything to the boys, but when I saw them showing up for dinner, I made a hasty check to be sure my demands had been met. And they had.

I tried this same tactic with my teenage sons' room. I left a card on the door stipulating they would receive no dinner till the room was cleaned. I signed it "The Management." One of my sons came home, read the sign, and went into his room with his books. Then he came out and asked what "the management" was serving for dinner. Luckily it was something he liked, or my plan could easily have failed. He might have preferred going without dinner to cleaning his room.

In one of our homes our front door entered onto a landing, with stairs going up and down from it. A wrought iron railing was by the stairs going down. During the winter, the children would come in, toss their coats on the railing, and head for the kitchen or bathroom. It was really unsightly. I told them repeatedly not to hang their coats on the railing, but they either conveniently forgot or chose to disobey. One day, trying to end my frustration, I made a sign and hung it on the front of the railing: "This is not a coat rack—5¢ for hanging." The children each had their own small allowance, and they enjoyed walking to a variety store on Saturdays to buy treats. I figured they wouldn't give up their Saturday adventure for a toss of a coat. And I was right.

When I was a child growing up, every time cross words were spoken, my mother would say, "Blessed are the peacemakers, for they shall be called the children of God." It really annoyed me when she said it. After I had children of my own, I could better appreciate her tactics. Still, I couldn't bring myself to use on my children those same words that had been a source of irritation to me. Neither could I tolerate arguing. Lacking any better solution, I simply sent the children to their rooms till they could come out and live peacefully with the rest of us.

Early in my marriage I didn't use the kind of restraint myself that I should have. I didn't argue with my children, but I did have a few serious disagreements with my husband. Perhaps my reading in the Book of Mormon, especially in 3 Nephi 11:29, that Satan was the father of all contention had some effect on me too. At any rate, I finally came to the conclusion that if I were ever to achieve peaceful unity in our family, I would have to set the example first myself. This wasn't easy. It seemed to be my second nature to want to retaliate. I learned that I had developed some bad habits that I needed help in overcoming. Knowing that what I had been doing was wrong just wasn't enough; I lacked the will I needed to change myself.

I sought the Lord's help. Sometimes I'd become discouraged when I fell back into old habits. Then I learned that I had to pray harder. I really learned through these experiences how quickly contention drives away the Spirit of the Lord. I began to pray privately and in family prayer that we could have more love and kindness in our home so that the Spirit of the Lord could abide there. I soon learned how futile it was to speak crossly and how humiliated it made me feel. I try always to apologize if I falter, for I hate having that ugly, sick spirit about me.

I have learned that we have two voices speaking to us from within: one from the Holy Ghost and one from Satan. It's up to us which one we choose to listen to. If we listen to Satan, we turn down the volume on what the Holy Ghost is saying to us. If we continually do this, the reception from the Holy Ghost is so poor that we can hardly hear it. The redeeming feature is that the opposite is true as well. If we listen to what the Holy Ghost tells us, Satan's volume is turned down. Then we only hear Satan on rare occasions. If we fall prey to Satan's tactics, the Holy Ghost will still prompt us what to do. For example, my husband may say something that hurts me and I may quickly retaliate. I have listened to Satan. I get a sick feeling in the pit of my stomach knowing I have done wrong. The Holy Ghost tells me to apologize. If I do, I feel better. If I don't, I still have that nagging feeling from within, but it becomes easier not to listen to it. Why should I apologize? He was the one who started it. Now I'm rationalizing and listening to Satan.

What would the Savior have me do? The answer is obvious: he would want me to make things right. In the first place, my husband most likely didn't mean to hurt me. Perhaps he had a bad day and didn't realize how his words sounded. At any rate, it only causes problems when I retaliate. I feel much better if I hold my tongue. And the reward is that there will still be peace in my home, and the Lord can abide there.

Once we have learned to better conquer self, it's easier to control the children. We become supersensitive to cross words, and they really hurt us.

We can't reason with an angry person, and we accomplish even less when both parties are angry. How much better it is to simply state that we're angry, and that we'll discuss this when we can do it calmly.

This is what I have done with my children. If there is an unpleasant moment between myself and a child, I send him to his room to think about it, saying, "We'll discuss it later when we can both be calm." If it's an unpleasant moment between the children, then they have to go to their rooms till they have conquered the ugly spirit they are displaying. Of course I never send two children to the same room. I have to separate them or I defeat my purpose.

Sometimes some of the children have been really stubborn and have spent a whole day in their rooms. Other times they hardly get there before they turn around and come back. On occasions when they return so hurriedly, they are arguing again within a couple of minutes. So back to their rooms they go. If this occurs more than twice, they are not to return till they get down on their knees and ask Heavenly Father to help them overcome their attitude.

It's almost amusing to see a child go to his room in a real temper and be back in less than two minutes with a smile on his face. A pleasant countenance is part of the rule to show that he is really sincere about trying to live peacefully.

If a child goes to his room and reads or does other things and seems to be content, I don't worry about it. He has to come out eventually, and when he does, he has to be cheerful or back he goes. At least while he's in there, he's not causing contention.

A few years ago I really wanted to teach the children how important it was for us to have the Lord's Spirit in our home. I wanted to do something specific to help prevent contention. Handling contention is one thing, but the ultimate, of course, is to prevent it from occurring in the first place. To help achieve this goal, I told our family the story Sister McKay told of how impressed she was when she first visited in President McKay's home. She noted particularly that the mother always spoke in a very soft voice—barely above a whisper. The children spoke softly too, so no loud voices were ever heard in their home.

After telling the story, I suggested that if we could all try this, I felt sure it would help us prevent contention from arising, and we would have a better chance of having the Lord's Spirit in our home. I challenged each of them to speak in a soft voice, and if anyone used a loud voice we should go up and very quietly say, "Oh, you forgot."

I felt very good about the way the children accepted the lesson. Our week was off to a good start. That week I had a really full schedule that became suddenly more full when an unexpected opportunity to can peaches came up. I wanted to get the canning out of the way as quickly as possible so I could get to other things, so I began as soon as I got the peaches home. Lacking counter space, I put the bottled peaches to cool on the dining room table, a trestle table that rested on shag carpeting. There were cases of fresh peaches on the table and some on the floor in front of the table. I had about six batches of bottled fruit cooling on the table when my children began arriving home from school. "Oh, goodie, peaches!" they exclaimed. One of the girls ran and climbed on the bench, put one hand on the table, and leaned over to get a peach out of the box on the table. The table wasn't well-balanced on the shag carpet anyway, and with the weight of the peaches on one side, all it took to tip the table was that little extra weight of her hand. Down all those peaches went, crashing to the floor. Under the shag carpeting was a cement floor. I stood there in dismay looking at all the broken glass, gooey peaches, and syrup all over my shag carpet, and tears sprang to my eyes. I put both hands on my head and said, "What am I going to do? What am I going to do now?" My little daughter came over, took hold of my pantleg, and said softly, "Oh, Mommie, you forgot."

It seems as though every time we venture out on a program of improvement, trials really come to thwart our progress. I knew I simply couldn't face that trauma right then. I left the house for a few minutes and then returned calm enough to handle the situation. My oldest daughter had gotten the shovel and was scooping up all the debris when I returned. All the children pitched in and we soon had it all cleaned up.

I really learned from that lesson. I could have become very upset with the daughter who caused the disaster, but what would it have accomplished? It would have created bad feelings in our home, and besides, it had been an accident. She never purposely would have done such a thing. I learned also that I could control my emotions if I really wanted to and made my mind up to do so. I didn't speak in a whisper, but neither did I raise my voice. I also found out that it only took a very few moments till I was calm enough to face the situation.

I have thought of the peach episode many times since. I have learned how much better it is to have unity and to work things out peacefully together than to say harsh things and destroy the spirit. The emotional climate of the home is really up to the mother. If she can learn to control herself and remain calm, she not only creates good feelings instead of bad, but she also sets an example for the children to follow. If she doesn't remain calm, she is also setting an example for the children to follow.

If children are to learn responsibility, they must be given choices. Even when my children were small, I always tried to let them make some decisions. I felt it was important that they develop the ability to decide for themselves. For example, I would go to the closet and say to one of my daughters, "Would you like to wear the blue dress or the red one today?" Often she'd say, "I want to wear the green one." Well, that wasn't in my original offer, and though it made little difference to me which dress she wore, I stuck to the offer I had given.

Now, it would be easier to select a dress and just put it on her, because once she had said she wanted to wear the green one, it might take a while to change her mind. Well, it is easier, but we tend to raise dependent children when we don't allow them to learn to make decisions. Children soon learn our nature and our way. If we give in to them, we're teaching them how to get their own way.

Giving children choices also helps prevent contention. For example, we may say: "Do you want to go to bed now or in ten minutes?" If we have previously given them choices and they have learned that we always stick with our offer, they will probably choose the "ten-minute" alternative. They might say: "I don't want to go to bed," but we simply state that that wasn't one of the choices, and repeat the offer. It usually only takes a few times till they learn the limits, but we must be consistent.

This system can be used in many different situations, and it will help avoid unpleasant circumstances. Perhaps I've prepared a tuna sandwich for a child for lunch, and he plays around with it but doesn't really eat it. Finally I become exasperated and tell him to hurry up and finish his lunch. He looks at it and states he's not hungry. I allow him to leave the table. Later in the afternoon I realize from his crankiness that he really was hungry. Perhaps he was just tired of tuna sandwiches. If I had given him a choice before I prepared lunch, he might have told me what appealed to him. For instance, I could have offered soup or a sandwich. He might have eagerly agreed to have soup. Then I could have offered two or three varieties from which to choose. He would have been able to make a decision, would have had something more appealing to him, and would have quickly consumed it. We mustn't forget, however, that some days children simply aren't hungry. I always figure that if a child doesn't eat at one meal, he'll probably be hungrier at the next, but I don't allow snacks in between if he has failed to eat the last meal.

From little simple choices children can grow to making more important ones. Parents can begin to include them in decisions involving the family—such as what to do for a vacation. My husband and I talk things over and allow the children to help make as many decisions as we feel we logically can. Every year I wanted to take my children to Disneyland, but every year they voted it down. Every year when we went to visit my sister in New Mexico, my husband wanted to drive off the main highway to see the Four Corners area, where Arizona, New Mexico, Colorado, and Utah all meet in one corner. It was about twenty miles out of our way. Every time he got voted down, however. Finally I took his side and told the children that their father was so good to take them on trips that perhaps they could let him see what he'd like to see. We voted again and he won. However, he missed the turnoff and didn't get to see it after all.

We have always asked the children for their ideas on the running of our household. They have given us good suggestions, and we have adopted many of them.

Sometimes when children get older, they may disagree with our decisions. This can become unpleasant if we don't handle the situation correctly. I have always made it a habit not to give a quick decision. I try to think it out before I answer so I won't have to change my mind. When there's a disagreement, however, I ask for their views. If I can see that I was wrong, I will change my mind. I tell them I was wrong and they were right. I am quick to add that because I have changed my mind once doesn't mean I ever will again. I don't want them coaxing me to change my mind. It wouldn't do any good anyway, as I won't change it unless I can see I was wrong.

On a few occasions I have made a decision and have stuck with it when the children have tried to persuade me that it was wrong. Later I have found out I was wrong. Perhaps I wasn't fully aware of the circumstance, or communication wasn't as clear as it should have been. At any rate, when I find I'm wrong, I go to the children and admit it. I've often told them that the Lord didn't send me to a parental school and give me a degree that said I knew all about being a parent. I let them know I'm still learning and likely to make many mistakes. And I've made many—particularly with my oldest daughter. I once told her she was like a guinea pig, and I was experimenting on her to learn how to be a parent. She was gracious with me because I didn't try to make her think I was perfect. I have made many mistakes and will probably make many more, but if we can talk it out and be honest, we can work out our problems. I really have been blessed with a special family. They are always willing to forgive me my mistakes and let me try again.

Chapter 10

Living with a Few Teenagers

On Father's Day in June 1962, my family gathered at my parents' home to honor my father. Kerry and Kyle were just a few weeks old, Debbie and Eric were two, and Beckie was four. I was constantly having to look after the children. I took a moment to catch my breath and sat down by my brothers, commenting about how nice it would be when our children were teenagers and could look after themselves. My brothers shook their heads and told me I'd better appreciate the situation while I had it so good. They informed me that the teenage years were by far the hardest for a parent. I looked at them in disbelief, thinking that it just couldn't be harder during the teenage years than it was right then.

People are different, and perhaps there's a reason for it. At any rate, I have had eight teenagers this year, and it has been the most glorious time of our lives. We are much closer than when they were small. It's not that I love them any more, but the ties are stronger. We understand one another better and can communicate on a more equal basis. They have grown mature and independent, but at the same time they have grown closer to us. Our love is based more on friendship now, whereas before it was more protective. These choice spirits have become such a part of me and my life that my trial now is seeing them leave the nest.

Through my many experiences with teenagers over the years, I have found that not all parents feel as I do. Shortly after we moved to Arizona I was asked to speak at the high school to two child growth and development classes. It wasn't my first experience with such a group, but it was my first experience speaking to a mostly non-Mormon group. I was terrified. I had had very little experience in mingling with nonmembers. I knew there'd be a communication problem. I went fasting, feeling urgently the need of the Lord's support and having a great desire to represent the Church well.

After I had been introduced and had spoken for a few minutes, the time was turned open for a question-and-answer period. Thank goodness there was a small podium in the classroom I could lean on to hold myself up. I was literally scared to death. A girl toward the center back of the room raised her hand. In a somewhat sarcastic tone she asked if my church *demanded* that we have large families. I replied that our church doesn't *demand* anything of us. Rather, we are free agents to do as we please. She came back sarcastically with, "Are you a Mormon?" I straightened proudly and answered in a kindly, determined tone, "Yes, I am." Her crusty demeanor seemed to crumple, and she offered no further outbursts.

The questions came pouring out. Did you know you were going to have multiple births? Did you gain a lot of weight? Did they cry a lot? How did you handle so many at once? Did you have a lot of help? And there were the usual questions about how many diapers, how much food, how did we afford it, and so forth.

Finally someone asked how we handled jealousy. The teacher had previously given me a list of sample questions that I might expect to be asked. This one had been on the list. I couldn't remember any occasions when we'd had jealousy, so I had talked to my husband about it. He couldn't recall any examples either, so I asked the children. They thought about it, but could not think of any situations in which jealousy had occurred. I told the class I had asked my family about jealousy, but no one could recall there ever having been any. That seemed to shock them.

They asked me about discipline and how we had handled that. I explained several of the programs we had used when the children were younger. Then one of the boys wanted to know how we handled discipline with our teenagers. It took me a while to explain that program. I told them how we tried to train our children to become independent. By the time they were fourteen, I said, we felt the children were old enough to be somewhat on their own. I explained that I'm a worrier and need to know where my children are at all times. However, I trust them completely, and they know this. After their fourteenth birthday, they no longer have to ask if they can go somewhere. We expect them to make their own decisions. We have spent their whole lives up to that point teaching them principles and standards that we'd like them to maintain. After they're fourteen, they're on their own to implement the teachings they have received. All we ask is that they keep us informed of their whereabouts so we don't worry.

Occasionally, after receiving this new freedom, some of the children have forgotten to tell us their plans. When they arrive home, they see the worried and frightened state in which they have put me. I'm quick to explain that I trust them, and they don't cause me a moment's worry in that regard. The thing I worry about is that they may have been in an accident riding their bikes and are lying hurt somewhere. I tell them that even though they know they're all right and can see no cause for concern, I simply don't know that. After a few such reminders, they have been good to tell us where they're going. Occasionally when I don't approve of where they're going or what they're doing, I tell them how I feel, but I never tell them they can't go.

After I had explained all this, the boy asked if, when the children got older, any of them had ever not told me where they were going. I told the class the following experience with our oldest son.

It was Friday evening, and my husband and I had been out together. We arrived home sometime before eleven o'clock, and I made the rounds of the bedrooms to make sure the girls were all home from babysitting before I locked the doors. As I passed by the boys' room, I noticed that Eric wasn't in his bed. I looked through the house and in the backyard for him. I couldn't find him anywhere. I wasn't too concerned, as he was on the high school track team and often did his running late at night when it was cooler. Being the worrier I am, however, I couldn't go to bed till I knew he was safely home. I worried that people driving cars might not see him as he ran along the edge of the road. I turned on the television while I waited for him. Shortly before midnight I heard him come in. "I sort of forgot to tell you where I was going, didn't I?" he stammered, as he came into the room. I looked at him and said, "Yes." He told me he had gone to the school ball game with some boys from the track team. They had gone out to eat afterwards. "Okay," I said, and off to bed he went.

When I finished telling the class, several asked questions at once. "Didn't you ground him?" "Didn't you take away his privileges?"

"No," I answered. He had never forgotten to tell me where he would be before, and having forgotten a few things myself, I couldn't be that harsh. I had no reason to believe he would ever forget again. His attitude wasn't belligerent; it was apologetic, and I knew he was sorry. He was sixteen at the time.

I could see the shock on the students' faces. I could hear comments about how differently their parents would have reacted. I went on to tell them that I had never grounded a child. I didn't think it a very good method of discipline. How was it related to the action that needed disciplining? If Eric had consistently left the house without telling me where he was going, I would have rescinded his right to leave without asking. That was related to the problem.

A few girls asked me if I would hire out as their mother. Some of the boys wanted to know if I'd give classes to teach their parents how to discipline teenagers. I realized then that youths outside the Church aren't really that much different from those in the Church. They all want to be loved and understood.

This feeling was further reinforced when one of the boys asked how we taught the teenagers to be so open with us. I looked at him and floundered momentarily. How could I tell him it was because of the gospel and the training they received? I finally told him that it was because we'd always loved them and stayed close to them. He wasn't satisfied with my answer and was quizzing me further when the bell rang. I have wished many times since that I had opened a door for him and replied simply that it was "the mark of Mormonism," or the mark of being raised in a Mormon home where gospel principles are taught.

Speaking at the high school was a challenging experience for me but also a learning one. Teenagers need time, love, and understanding from their parents. Too often parents are so busy doing other things that the children suffer. In order to salve their consciences, many parents lavish material gifts on their children. They think this will make their children happy and feel close to the parents. Material items, however, simply don't bring lasting happiness.

My years of teaching youth have given me many insights that could be helpful to parents. One of the main things girls this age want from their parents is for the parents to listen to them. This is always the biggest complaint: "My parents don't listen to me."

Girls have often approached me with problems and asked my advice on how to handle them. I suggest that they talk the problems over with their parents. Usually they laugh sarcastically and say, "They wouldn't listen to me." I then suggest that perhaps they are using the wrong approach. I tell them to approach their parents softly, kindly, and ask for an appointment with them when they can sit and talk calmly without having to worry about interruptions. Many do try this, and some succeed. Others report that their parents simply do not have time to listen to them.

Too often in our lives we fail to give heed to the most important things. We get so caught up in trying to fulfill assignments that we fail to really live the gospel. What could possibly be more important to parents than to bring their children unto Christ—to teach them to love him, to help them find out for themselves that he lives, that he gave himself as a willing sacrifice so that they might once again live with their Heavenly Father. Children need parents who have time—time to listen, time to play, time to understand, time to love. Our first and primary assignment is our children. Nothing should be as important to parents as these special spirits who have been entrusted to their care. No committee meeting, lesson to teach, board meeting, council meeting, or talk to prepare should take precedence over our families. And yet, each of us at one time or another has probably pushed our children into the background while rushing to do some less important task. We all have many church assignments and responsibilities, but our number one priority should be our children. Remember President McKay's counsel: "No other success in life can compensate for failure in the home."

When parents fail to listen to their children and to spend time with them, they're essentially saying to the children, "You're not as important to me as . . ." Two things then may happen. The children may withdraw and keep everything to themselves, or they might find someone else who does have time for them and will listen to them.

It isn't healthy or wise for a child to withdraw within himself. Teenagers particularly need advice. They need someone to whom they can turn for help and comfort during these frustrating years when they are neither child nor adult. If they have no one, they suffer through many things in silence. So often this suffering is needless, and could be eliminated, if they only had someone with a little more experience, a little more maturity, to guide them.

If a child turns to someone other than the parent in his time of need, he gets counseling and the comfort he needs, but is it the kind that the parents would approve of? In addition, the other person gets the love and confidence that should have been bestowed upon the parent. The close association that could have been enjoyed between parent and child is forfeited—a spiritual bond forsaken.

Too often parents, laden with the guilty realization that they are neglecting their children, turn to other sources to win their children's devotion. They give them material things in place of time. A child, inexperienced and unknowing, gleefully accepts the monetary reward, for it brings fleeting happiness. Even he doesn't realize that that isn't what he really wants. Soon the pleasure derived from the new toy, new dress, or new bicycle is gone, and he is unhappy again. The parent, in his guilt (whether he realizes it or not), buys something else to make up for time not given. Again the child is pacified for a time. As the child grows older his need for material goods as a source of happiness increases. The parent begins to feel that the child is taking advantage of him. Then the material goods, instead of bringing parent and child closer together, cause a greater chasm between them. Sometimes the gulf becomes so large it is never bridged. Neither parent nor child ever seems to consciously realize that what the child really wanted was the parent's time.

For some reason, outsiders seem to analyze this problem far more quickly than does the parent or the child. The child doesn't really know what he wants, other than to be happy. The problem is that he isn't mature enough to know what will bring that happiness. He needs parents wise enough and kind enough to give him what he needs instead of lavishing him with the material goods he asks for, which really aren't for his good.

For example, one Christmas we decided to buy our son a 35-millimeter slide camera for his mission. At Thanksgiving, when he was home from school, my husband casually brought up the subject of cameras. He found out that our son had done some investigating and had decided on a certain type of camera that he wanted—quite an expensive one. We were in a quandary because we hadn't planned on spending that much for a camera, but we looked around and finally found a price we considered to be a good buy for that model. After talking it over for nearly an hour at the store, we finally decided that keeping our son in the mission field for even two months would have cost more than the camera, and we had been relieved of this responsibility because of our son's initiative and savings program. So we decided to purchase the camera, as well as more expensive gifts than usual for the other children so no one would feel hurt. We were quite excited at Christmas because this was the first time we had purchased such extravagant gifts for the children.

When the children came home from college, I heard our son, who was saving for the mission, casually ask his sister what she would like for Christmas that didn't cost anything. She told him to write her a poem.

When Christmas morning dawned, I was as excited as a little child again. That morning we had our special traditional Christmas program. Our son read the narration, and we all sang Christmas carols at intervals in the program. It was a beautiful occasion, and everyone was happy. I could hardly wait for the presents to be handed out. It had meant much to me, and I'm sure to their father, to have purchased for our children such special gifts that year. I was all caught up in their enjoyment of their gifts when our oldest daughter started to unwrap a very flat, thin present. Her brother cautioned her as she somewhat carelessly tore into it. Inside was a piece of paper with writing on it. She looked at it briefly and then said, somewhat baffled, "It's in German." She looked at her brother questioningly and handed it to him. "Read it," she said. He began very softly. As he read in German, emotion crept into his voice, and though I couldn't understand what he was saying, I felt the spirit with which it was read, and tears sprang to my eyes. As he finished, his voice broke and his sister asked him to translate the poem. He began again in English, and as the words were unfolded, all our hearts seemed to be as one. The poem was about a sister and what she is—written from a special brother's viewpoint. He had a difficult time finishing because of his emotions. When he did finish, his sister sprang to her feet and ran to him. He stood and they embraced and wept together. Love flooded the room and tears flowed freely. In the midst of a room filled with expensive material gifts, it was the gift that cost no money and came from the heart that had indeed brought the greatest pleasure.

Chapter 11

Cutting the Apron Strings

Many people have asked how we have been able to cut the apron strings by the time our children are fourteen. We believe in two theories. First, from the Prophet Joseph Smith, "I teach them correct principles, and they govern themselves." We feel very strongly that his statement applies to our family as well as it did to the members of the Church when Joseph Smith uttered it. The children haven't always done as I would have wanted them to, but the decisions have belonged to them, not to me. And maybe by the time they are fully matured, they will do things differently.

Second, I was very familiar with how Joseph F. Smith, sixth president of the Church, was called on a mission to the Sandwich Islands at age fifteen. The Prophet Joseph Smith was receiving revelation at age fourteen. Mormon was called by Ammaron at the age of ten to be responsible for the vast accumulation of Nephite records. He was also to remember the things that he saw and to make a record of them. By the time he was fifteen he had seen the Savior, and at age sixteen he was given the awesome responsibility of commanding the whole Nephite army. I figured that if the Lord thought fourteen- , fifteen- , and sixteen-year-olds were old enough for this kind of responsibility, then I could certainly train my children to be responsible by the same age—with the Lord's help. Besides, they would be leaving home in four more years and would really be on their own. I wanted their first experiment with independence to be while we were still around to analyze and give counsel and advice. I felt very impressed that children couldn't reach responsible independence if we were always making their decisions or forcing them. I didn't want to raise dependent children, and I felt the authoritarian approach would cause them to be that way.

When my children began approaching their teenage years, I

became quite concerned about being able to guide them through those frustrating, trying years without their having to learn things the hard way as I had done. I didn't know exactly what to do or where to seek help. I began thinking about families whose children had turned out well. My older sister's children seemed almost perfect to me. Gerald's older sister's boys had turned out to be just what I wanted my boys to be. I determined to ask both of them their secrets for success.

When I approached my sister, she didn't even hesitate. She said parents should train their children the very best they can when the children are little. When they reach their teenage years, the parents become their counselors. They advise the youths, but the youths make their decisions.

When we made a trip to Calgary again, I approached Gerald's sister with the same question. She replied that parents should keep the doors of communication open, and they shouldn't lower their standards.

Communicating with teenagers doesn't really require learning a new language. What it does require is listening and understanding and loving. Does our teenager know that we love him? If not, that may be the root of our problem. A teenager must feel loved in order to be open enough to communicate with parents. Do we trust him? That is also a necessary prerequisite to good communication. As Goethe states, "If you treat a man as he is, he will remain as he is, but if you treat him as if he were what he ought to be, and could be, he will become what he ought to be, and should be." If we don't love him, he'll act hateful. If we don't trust him, he'll respond in a like manner. We can't just pretend to trust either; we must trust him sincerely in order for him to respond favorably.

Some people may argue that trust must be earned. I agree. But before trust can be earned, it must be taught. And where and when is it taught? In the home, by the parents, from the time the children are born. If the proper groundwork for communicating hasn't been laid in a child's life, when he or she reaches the teenage years there will be little hope for open communication.

It has been mentioned that listening, loving, and trusting are some ways we can keep the doors of communication open. Some door-closers are judging, overreacting, not listening, and failing to understand.

Too often parents see only their side in a problem situation.

Too often they respond with "I am the parent. I know what's right or best under the circumstances. I insist on being obeyed." This type of parent never stops to analyze logically. He uses methods that Satan was wont to use in our premortal state. Those methods were unacceptable to the Lord then, and I'm sure they are now.

The Lord doesn't want us to force our children to do what's right. He wants us to love them into the right way. We should be gentle and kind when we're trying to be persuasive, never dogmatic and abusive.

One of the most important things in understanding teenagers is to really see the situation from their point of view. Remember how we felt at the same age. Remember the old Indian saying: try walking in their moccasins. This can best be achieved in three steps: (1) listen, (2) listen, and (3) listen!

Listening isn't a passive thing where only our ears are involved. Listening entails much more. It requires concentrating on what is being said, then repeating back to the teenager, in our own words, what has been said to make sure we understand. If we will do this, our teenager will realize that we really are trying to understand his point of view. He will begin to relax and to be even more open. If at any time we react with a judgment, he will clam up again and close the door.

Many times a teenager will be very cautious. He may not trust us completely at first and may partially withhold things from us. Parents need to be clever enough to be able to read between the lines. What the child is saying may not be the problem at all. By carefully scrutinizing the situation, we may be able to determine where or what the real problem is.

For instance, when I was in eighth grade I became quite cranky. Sometimes I'd be very quiet and sullen. After several days of such behavior, one night my father in exasperation asked me what was wrong. All I said, in great big sobs, was that I wanted to go live with the neighbors. Well, my father reacted to the situation and punished me. The result was that the door for communication between us closed, and I never reopened it until after I was married. He tried several times to reopen it, but I simply didn't respond.

Now let's analyze what I really was saying to him. (I didn't understand this at the time, but I have since been able to comprehend it.) What I really was saying was that I was unhappy at home. If he had pursued this area, perhaps between us we could have figured out what was causing my unhappiness and might have rectified it.

Looking back on the situation, I think perhaps I needed more acceptance and attention. The neighbors, who were also my employers, treated me kindly and lovingly. They praised me, and I felt accepted by them. In my own home I was a middle child. I had an older sister who was very accomplished musically and had an outgoing personality. She had many friends, and everything she did seemed to be just right. My older brother was the apple of my father's eye. I didn't blame my father—I adored my brother too. I was so proud to go to junior high in the same school building that housed the high school because my brother would be there. Imagine how crushed I was when he told me not to speak to him at school because he didn't want anyone to know I was his sister. Add to this the fact that my parents were very active in their church assignments as well as had a large farm to run. My mother was also an avid genealogist, and this kept her quite busy.

None of my six brothers or sisters felt neglected or unloved. I was the only one. I was supersensitive and took to heart literally everything that was said to me. Little things built up into big things, and I became unhappy.

During this period in my life, I spent a great deal of time walking along the lake that bordered our ranch. Here it was peaceful and serene, with snowcapped mountains majestically rising in the background. How often I would talk to my beautiful mountain as I walked around the lake. The Indians called her "the sleeping lady" because of her shape. In my innocence and youth, I talked to her as I would to no one else. She always had time to listen and really seemed to care. I'm afraid I spent too much time fantasizing at this time in my life. It became so easy to pretend and let my imagination run wild. I could become almost oblivious to my parents' presence, even as they were talking to me. I'm sure this was a trial for them. I wish we could have sat down calmly and talked out my problems—perhaps even I would have understood them then. But that didn't seem to be the school of thought in those days.

I know a girl who had a trying period in her life in her middle teenage years. Often she would make a comment about how fat she was or how ugly she was. She was neither fat nor ugly—in fact, quite the opposite. Her parents tried to reassure her, but it seemed to fall on deaf ears, and she'd end up running to her room in tears. After a few weeks of her acting this way, her mother finally realized the root of the problem. The mother, unable to sleep one night, had been thinking about her daughter's unusual behavior. Suddenly the truth had hit her as surely as though someone had poured a bucketful of pure inspiration over her head.

Despite the late hour, she arose from her bed and went to her daughter's room. She awakened her daughter and told her she now knew what had been bothering her. She told her daughter that her fear of being ugly and fat really hadn't been the problem at all; what was bothering her was that she was not dating. The mother asked her daughter if that weren't the case. The daughter nodded her head as big tears welled up in her eyes.

The mother put her arms around her daughter. The door to communication had been opened. The mother had understood. Her daughter, weeping openly, said she never would have told her mother if she hadn't guessed what was wrong. Now that she knew her mother understood, she told her how hard it was to sit and listen to the other girls talk about their dates. She always felt out of place.

The mother listened and the daughter talked. It seemed a reservoir had been opened that needed to run dry as the daughter talked on and on. The mother responded with warmth, love, and understanding. The problem wasn't solved instantly, but it was made more bearable because two shared the burden. The wound had been opened, the infection allowed to run out, and the sore thoroughly washed. Now all that was needed was time for healing.

Parents can often doctor the spirit of a wounded teenager. The approach must be cautious, however, lest irreparable damage is inflicted.

One day two of my teenage sons came home and informed me their brother had been dismissed as manager of the track team. Apparently he had missed track practice, which had been early that day since a meet had been cancelled. The coach, who was upset at his absence, dismissed him as manager of the team. I felt quite discouraged. One of the things I had always tried to teach my children was to be dependable. I wondered how I had failed in this regard with this son. To not show up for a track practice when you were the manager was unforgivable, I felt. I didn't blame the coach for dismissing him: I was upset with him too.

He was late coming home that night. We were halfway through dinner when he walked in. As soon as he was in sight, I lit into him, verbally tearing him apart. I had raised him to be dependable, how could he act in such an irresponsible manner, and so forth. He stood with his eyes downcast and took all I dished out. When I was through, he headed for his room. I told him to sit down and eat or dinner would be cold.

"I'm not hungry," he retorted as he slammed his bedroom door.

I sat at the table not believing what I had just done. I had done everything I had always preached against. I, who loved teenagers with all my heart, had just muffed it. I had not only reacted—I had judged, and I certainly hadn't listened. "Well, perhaps it's not too late," I thought.

I sent one of the younger children to tell my son I wanted to talk to him. I knew he didn't want to come out, but he was obedient. I asked him to sit down on the opposite side of the table, where I could observe his reactions. "I don't want to eat," he said. I told him I just wanted to talk to him. He sat down.

I told him I had handled the situation poorly. I had done everything I'd always told parents not to do. I hoped he would give me a second chance. I asked him if we could start over as though nothing had happened. He was much more lenient with me than I had been with him.

I told him I was ready to listen and would like to hear his side of the story. He began opening up. When the track meet was cancelled he had gone to a friend's house to help him with a paper that he didn't understand. Time had slipped by and he was late for the practice. When he did arrive, the coach was very upset with him and dismissed him. I asked if he hadn't told the coach why he wasn't there. He didn't think it would have mattered.

My son really admired the coach, and they had been the best of friends. I could see how hurt my son was, as tears spilled silently down his face. I went over to him, put my arms around him, and asked if he didn't think it would be a good idea if he went and apologized to the coach. He didn't think it would do any good, as he was sure the coach wouldn't take him back.

I agreed that he probably wouldn't get the job back again, but suggested that something more was at stake than being manager of the track team. He looked at me quizzically. I explained that the most important thing was his friendship with the coach. He agreed, but wanted to know what he could do. I suggested he go and apologize to the coach. He said the coach probably wouldn't think it was a good excuse. I agreed, and told him the coach would probably feel that it was my son's responsibility to find out when the practice was and to be there. He should have assumed that it would have been held right after school since the meet had been cancelled.

I told my son I thought he should go to the coach and tell him he was sorry for not being there and for disappointing him. I told him not to alibi or to try to get the job back. I urged him to simply apologize and let the coach know how much he valued his friendship.

My son sat and thought about it. Finally, he shook his head and sobbed, "I can't do it; I just can't do it."

I reasoned with him again, and he agreed that his friendship with the coach was of the utmost importance to him. He simply lacked the courage to go and apologize: the spirit was willing but the flesh was weak. I asked him if he didn't think the Lord would help him. He said he knew He would, but it was so hard.

I turned and asked his sister if she would drive him over to the coach's house and wait while he went in. She was willing. I literally half-pulled and half-dragged my son out to the car. All the time he was sobbing that he couldn't do it.

I paced the floor and prayed while they were gone. Soon my son walked in the front door standing tall and erect, his eyes glistening and a smile on his face. He had accomplished his goal. Truly all was well again. Relief flooded my soul as I asked what had happened.

My daughter informed me that it was a sheer miracle he even got out of the car. One of the coach's children came out of the house and saw him, so my son finally went to the door. The coach loves youth and is truly big and kindhearted. He not only forgave my son but was willing to give him another chance. Their friendship is still intact.

I often shudder as I think of what the outcome could have been that day if I hadn't come to my senses when I did. The door of communication with my son would certainly have been closed. How long it would have remained closed is anyone's guess: it might have been forever. Also, a priceless friendship could have been lost. Yet today my son still admires the track coach. They are the greatest of friends. What a loss it would have been to my son to sever that friendship.

Another thing parents often do that stifles communication is to overreact and display shock. A shocked expression or attitude can quickly close the communication door. I guess I had a real advantage in this area: having been quite wild as a teenager myself, and having taught teenagers for several years, nothing they said or did could cause me to display a shocked reaction. It wasn't that I was never shocked—I simply had learned to control it so well that they didn't know I was shocked.

On one occasion my daughter's sixth grade teacher sent her, for the third time that year, out into the hall for being noisy. He was quite exasperated with her. He told her that if she misbehaved again, he would have to call her mother. My daughter looked at him unabashed and told him her mother already knew. The teacher was shocked.

I was aware of my daughter's action, as she had said. She knew I disapproved; however, she was not punished for her actions. She knew I would not stick up for her at school, and she would have to suffer the consequences there. I had also pointed out the folly of such behavior. We had talked it out calmly and without judgmental reaction. She felt free to discuss all her activities with me.

I have always been very open with my children. They know of my past life and many of my experiences as a teenager. I have been open with them in hopes that they could learn from my experiences without having to go through similar experiences themselves. They know of occasions when I sluffed school. They know of times I was disrespectful to my teachers. They know the consequences I suffered from such actions.

I want my children to be honest and frank with me. I tell them that if they ever want to sluff school, I want them to call me first. If they misbehave in school, I want to hear it from them first, not from a school official. In short, I want to hear of all their activities—good or bad.

Pursuant to my instructions, one of my daughters called me one day to inform me she was planning to cut a class with several other girls. Her friends thought she was really crazy when she insisted on calling me before going with them. I appreciated her call and told her I disapproved of her plans. I tried to tell her she'd end up in trouble if she went through with her plans. She decided to go and suffer the consequences.

The consequences turned out to be rather severe. The teacher had planned a surprise quiz for that hour she was gone.

Later, after their absence was reported, the girls were called into the office. The assistant principal talked to them and asked each girl where she had been. Most of the girls invented excuses that were accepted. They were allowed to make up the exam. Our daughter told the truth and was not allowed to make up the exam.

We had always tried to teach our children to be honest. In situations such as these you always hope they'll be truthful, but it seemed a hard lesson to tell the truth and be punished while others lied and were not punished. I was afraid this was a lesson that could teach a child to go in the wrong direction. My husband and I finally decided we'd better go to the school and talk with the officials. We felt we should at least stick up for our daughter, as she had been truthful. My husband thought we could divulge some of the circumstances, but we were careful not to disclose the names of the other girls involved nor the fabrications they had invented.

Finally, after we had had a long, drawn-out discussion with the assistant principal, he began to understand the problem. At first he seemed to think we had given our daughter permission to sluff because she had called home before sluffing. He went into a lengthy discussion of how parents didn't have any right to keep a child out of school. If we were persistent in allowing our children to miss school, he would have to turn us over to the county attorney's office for prosecution.

After coming back to the pertinent issue of punishing our daughter for being honest (while others who had done the same thing and lied about it were allowed to go scot-free), the assistant principal finally said he would discuss the situation with the teacher. If the teacher decided to let our daughter make up the test or receive partial credit, the assistant principal would go along with it.

When the teacher was apprised of the details of the situation, he was more than cooperative. Our daughter had been a good student, and he was willing to give her another chance. He realized there was more at stake than a mere math grade.

Needless to say, our daughter learned a great lesson from this episode. And thanks to an understanding math teacher, she learned that it is still best to be honest. After the whole experience was ended, she could go on with a clear conscience and forget it. However, she was never tempted to sluff again.

One day a teenage boy dropped by our home and asked if I

would cut his hair. As it was quite long, I was delighted to oblige. I found out during the process that he didn't want nearly as much off as I was willing to remove. But the important thing about that haircut was our conversation. He told me many things he had been doing that were wrong. As I came around to cut the front of his hair, he asked me if I weren't shocked. I looked him straight in the eye and told him I'd lived too long and had seen too much and he couldn't tell me anything that would shock me.

Then he really opened up and told me his innermost feelings. He had come from a home where his parents hadn't been very active in the Church. Some of his friends were good members of the Church; some weren't members at all. He told me about some of his escapades: drugs, liquor, and nights in jail. He told me how his parents really didn't seem to care. Then he said the most shocking thing—that he'd really like to go on a mission. He said he knew he didn't have the strength and courage to live so he could do so unless someone helped him.

I put my arms on his shoulders, looked him in the eye again, and told him I cared. I would help him. The Lord cared. He loved him and would help him. My heart ached for the boy. How I wished I could have taken him into my home and given him the love and strength he needed. A few days later my daughter came home from school and told me his parents had kicked him out and he had left the state.

I have thought so often about that boy. He would never have opened up and talked to me if I had appeared shocked at the things he was divulging to me. Trust and open communication came after he saw I wasn't overreacting or judging. How could I judge? I had done too many things wrong myself to stand in condemnation of someone else.

This boy felt no one loved him. How had he gone so far in life without feeling any love? Had everyone always judged him and withheld the one thing he needed to change his life? What miracles love and understanding can achieve—and what destruction shock, overreacting, and judging can cause! How cautious we, as parents, need to be! I feel we will be judged for our actions with these precious souls God has sent to our homes. How they turn out depends, in a large measure, on us. How are we *reacting* to our responsibilities?

I remember the first time I thought much about overreacting. I had attended June Conference where in one session we were instructed by a Salt Lake City judge. He told about coming home from work one night and walking into his teenage daughter's room. There were pictures of the Beatles everywhere—even all over the ceiling. He yelled for her to come to her room quickly; he was going to have this mess cleaned up right now! By the time she got there, he had calmed down somewhat, and was able to talk to her about all her pictures. She was really excited about the Beatles. During their discussion, however, he decided it was just a phase she was going through, and that he could live with it for a while. So he said nothing about taking the pictures down, and a few months later she got rid of the pictures on her own. She had outgrown that phase. He pointed out that had he overreacted and insisted that the pictures go, it might have created a gulf in their relationship.

A few months after I heard this discussion, our oldest daughter went into a bubble-gum-chewing stage that was very annoying to her father. It didn't bother me, but my husband was quick to remind me I had been a gum-chewer when he married me, so it was easier for me to understand. I told him of the class I'd been to during June Conference, and suggested that if we didn't overreact she'd probably outgrow it. If we attacked her, it might reinforce the habit. He decided to overlook her habit and not overreact. A few months later the bubble-gum phase had ended. We learned from this experience to overlook as many of these little incidentals to growing up as we could without permanently harming the child.

We are taught through the scriptures not to judge others. Yet how often do we as parents set aside this admonition of the Savior? How often have you heard "How could you do such a thing? We certainly never trained you that way," or some similar statement? It seems teenagers often get this type of reaction in their homes. I have heard many such reports from working with teenagers over the years. How much better it would be if parents could accept the mistakes teenagers make and help them instead of criticizing them. What better moment could a parent find to teach his children the principle of repentance and how to find the way back? I saw a perfect example of this once, and it so impressed me that I have never forgotten it.

I was standing in line at our ward library waiting to get some materials I needed to teach my Sunday School class. A young girl was standing in line in front of me. Then her boyfriend's father came into the building, and, seeing her, walked up, put his arm around her, and welcomed her into the family. It was then that I noticed the engagement ring on her finger. After he left, I congratulated her and spoke to her briefly. She had received the ring the night before. I asked her when they were planning to be married, knowing that her fiance was of an age to go on a mission and knowing also how much his mother wanted him to go. I was quite surprised when she said, "Next month." I knew the mother must be hurt, but I didn't think much more about it.

About two weeks later their wedding invitation arrived. I noticed the words "married in the —— temple" were not on the invitation, but passed it off, thinking the printer had made a mistake. We attended the wedding reception, and it was a beautiful, happy occasion. Much later I heard the groom's mother talking about the trouble the young people were in. It was the first time the thought even entered my mind that something might be amiss. Later, when circumstances indeed did prove that things weren't as they should have been, I couldn't help remembering the affectionate scene between the man and his future daughter-in-law. There was no ugly scene, no weeping, no "how could you's." Instead there was a simple, calm (at least on the outside) acceptance.

I had an occasion to mention to this very special father-in-law my admiration of the magnificent manner in which he had reacted to such a heartbreaking situation. I was even more amazed at his reply. He asked what else he could have done but accept it. The young people had made a mistake. All the criticizing in the world wouldn't take it away. "They need more help, more love, more understanding than ever before," he confided.

I couldn't help shedding tears as I spoke to that gracious man. How blessed indeed were those young people to have such a parent! How many more teenagers would make it to a successful life if more parents could react in such a manner!

Because of this fine example, I was able to react more favorably in a trying situation. I had told my fifteen-year-old son repeatedly that if he left his ten-speed bicycle parked in front of the house instead of putting it away in the garage, it would be stolen. One day a sister in the ward told me how her daughter's ten-speed had been stolen in the middle of the day while she was babysitting. She had hidden the bike in the bushes, too. I told my son about this, hoping to reinforce what I had already told him, and warned him again about leaving his bike out.

About ten days later, on Saturday, my husband and I had been away all day, and when we arrived home about 9:30 that evening, one of the younger children told us our son's bike had been stolen. He had left it out by the front doorway. It had been taken in the middle of the afternoon. Our son had gone to a stake dance, so there was no opportunity to discuss it with him. My husband asked him about it the next morning and found out he had called the police. He had also searched all over the neighborhood but, of course, had found nothing.

All that day I went about my duties as normally as possible, and never mentioned the bike to my son. The next morning I fixed his sack lunch and sent him off to school. He came home that evening and we had dinner. Still nothing was said. During family home evening, he finally brought up the subject and asked if I weren't ever going to say something to him. I looked at him and said simply, "You had a choice. You made a decision, and now you'll have to suffer the consequences of that decision."

Actually, I was heartsick over the loss of the bike. I think it hurt me much more than it hurt him. It was a hard lesson, but nothing I could say would bring the bicycle back. He had chosen to ignore my advice and had suffered a loss. It was his decision and he would have to live with it. I tried not to judge him. I knew having to walk would help him learn a lesson, and not being able to do all the things his friends did might have some effect on him too. No punishment was administered. He suffered through natural consequences.

Becoming responsible sometimes involves some hard lessons—trials for both the child and his parents. But through communication, trust, and understanding, the lessons can be learned, the doors opened, and the pathway to mutual respect and love made clear.

Chapter 12

The Facts of Life

One thing that I have noticed that causes a gap between parents and children is sex education—or perhaps I should say the lack of it. My experience working with teenage girls has borne out the fact time and time again that girls who feel free to discuss sex with their mothers have a good relationship with them. Girls who don't feel free to discuss sex with their mothers don't discuss other things with them freely either.

It is a sad circumstance when sex cannot be discussed freely between parents and children, because home is where this kind of education belongs. Many schools make an attempt at teaching it, and for those who receive no instruction anywhere else, this is of some value. But I'd hate to leave the instruction of such an important topic up to any assigned teacher. There are few people I would trust to teach the real doctrine and sacredness of sex to my children. I am against such things being taught in the public schools, except perhaps basic physiology.

But parents protest that they are not qualified to teach such things to their children. Over their protests I would say that any way they might teach this subject would be more appropriate than having it come from someone else. There are many books available to aid parents who feel inadequate; some have even been written by members of the Church. With such help as this, and guidance from the Lord, there is no excuse for parents failing to instruct their children. They shouldn't feel that they have to have a knowledge of physiology to teach their children. Rather, they should trust in the Lord to guide them; use the terms and phraseology he puts into their minds; teach the sacred, spiritual aspect of sex; and teach their children it is something so special and sacred that it should only be discussed in their family. If parents are open and frank with their children, the children will love and respect them for it.

The time to answer a question is when it is asked. I have always tried to answer anything the children asked when they asked it. I don't believe in putting them off, telling them I'll explain later. They may never ask again. We should answer when they ask. If we don't feel satisfied with the way we have handled the question, we can always say we'll discuss it again later after the children have had time to think about it. Then we should always remember to bring it up again later and supplement our earlier teachings.

Our situation was a little different from the average. When we brought the triplets home from the hospital, our six- and four-year-olds wanted to know why we had two and three babies at a time while other people only had one.

When our children asked why we had multiple births, I told them about how there are tiny eggs within the mother that can become babies if fertilized by the father. (They didn't ask how the eggs were fertilized at that time, so I didn't volunteer the information. I answered only what they had asked.) These eggs are stored right here, I would say, pointing to each side of my abdomen. I explained that usually only one egg comes down each month where it can be fertilized and grow into a baby. I then told the children that we had two or three babies because that many eggs came down and were fertilized. I really didn't say too much more about it at the time, and they were satisfied.

A couple of years later when they asked me how Daddy fertilized the eggs, this was the proper time to go into the sacred union between husband and wife—how it was ordained of God and brought a special, spiritual love between mother and daddy. At this time they were cautioned against ever talking to their friends or others about it. It was something we discussed together as a family. I told them their father and I would answer any questions they had, so they should always come to us to talk about their concerns. We never separated the girls from the boys when sex was being discussed.

What if children never ask any questions? Many mothers have presented this problem to me. From experiences with my own children, and from listening to their discussions of other children, I have concluded that if a child hasn't asked any questions by the time he's eight years old, it's time for us to give him some basic instruction. Some parents may feel this is too young, but the Lord set the age eight as the time when children are accountable. We don't have to tell them everything at this age—

just a few basics. If we've given these few basics, the children will come to us when questions arise. Otherwise, far too often, they will discuss the subject with others at school. When this happens, we can never be sure what concepts they are getting. I would prefer to fill their minds with good basic principles of sex rather than to have their minds polluted with the misinformation that is passed around at school.

We shouldn't ever be embarrassed when discussing sex with our children. If we are, we just might close a communication door that may never be reopened. It is our duty as parents to teach our children. If we hesitate, waiting to teach them until they're older than eight, we may be dismayed to discover that someone else has already done the job for us—and irreparable damage may have been inflicted during the teaching. My heart aches for children who have sex presented to them in a crude, harsh manner. This could easily be avoided if parents would assume the responsibility to teach their own children.

Several years ago Elder Mark E. Petersen spoke in general conference about sex education, saying that it should be taught in the home. I had had some related discussions in previous Mutual classes. Because of this, each new class that came in was informed by the older girls about our special night. Then the new girls would want to know when we would be having it again. After Elder Petersen's talk I was very hesitant about even approaching the subject, but after much pressure from the girls, I finally went and discussed it with the bishop. When he was apprised of the severe lack of knowledge on the part of the girls, he decided I should go on with our special nights. He cautioned me about approaching the subject from a sacred, spiritual viewpoint, and I assured him that I always did so. I wished he could have been present without the girls knowing it, for I know he would have been satisfied. The saddest thing I learned from ten years of teaching Laurels was that very few girls felt they could freely discuss sex with their mothers. Most of the girls felt that their mothers were embarrassed, and this made them uncomfortable.

Mutual girls would sometimes ask me to go to special mother-daughter nights at the high school with them because their mothers wouldn't go. I was delighted to go, but felt the mother was the loser. One high school asked a local doctor to come and show a film he had made of the actual birth of a baby. I attended with two of my Mutual girls. It was very informative, and I appreciated seeing it, especially as it opened up new areas of discussion between us. I was thrilled to share this special experience with the girls, but also sad that their mothers had chosen to miss such an opportunity. Their decision had cheated them of a special experience with their daughters that would have helped create or maintain a close relationship.

On another occasion I was invited by one of my own daughters to spend an afternoon at school, where the school nurse would be showing a special film for the girls. It was related to their maturing and beginning their menstrual periods. I walked into the school that day with a woman from our ward. She commented about how grateful she was that the school was showing the film, for it would open up the opportunity for a discussion with the girls. I guess my shocked expression caused her to ask if I didn't agree. I told her my daughter already knew about as much as I did—she was over twelve years old. Now it was her turn to be shocked. "My, you are a good mother," she said. Later that afternoon I asked my daughter if that mother's daughter had ever discussed sex-related subjects. My daughter informed me the girl knew all there was to know. I felt so sad to feel that another mother had missed a golden opportunity for teaching and communicating with her daughter.

One lesson that surprised the girls in my Mutual classes was how the way the girls dress has an effect on boys. No one had ever told them that. Many of the girls wondered why their mothers had let them dress in miniskirts, sleeveless tops, tight sweaters, and other revealing attire. I had wondered that myself. Mothers know the effect on boys their daughters will have if they are dressed in an inappropriate manner. I can't imagine a mother, much less a father, ever wanting a boy to look at her daughter in such a manner.

When I attended Brigham Young University, our home teacher, a returned missionary, gave us a lesson on proper dress standards. He told us about the most beautiful girl he had ever seen. He said she was wearing a wedding dress that had a high neckline and long sleeves and touched the floor. It would have been almost impossible for her to have been covered more, and yet this was the most beautiful girl he had ever seen. He then told us that good boys don't appreciate girls who are scantily clad. They may look at girls who are dressed inappropriately, but they don't respect them. I repeated this story each year to my Mutual class. I have wanted so often to tell mothers to guard their girls, to protect them. Dress them appropriately. Safeguard their purity! Don't help them throw it away.

Sex doesn't have to be discussed just between mother and daughter or father and son. In fact, we have devoted family home evenings to the subject. Sometimes we have discussed it with all the children together. Sometimes I have discussed it with just the older children.

On one occasion I was talking openly with the five older children. Gerald had taken the four younger girls to a separate room. At the end of our discussion the children were talking openly and asking questions freely. This was shortly after our move from Utah to Arizona, and I was soon to discover that my children and I had lived a sheltered life in a Mormon community. Being out in the world was truly a different experience. One of my younger sons asked the meaning of a certain word. I had never heard the word and was shocked when my older son was able to answer him. I asked where he had gained that bit of information. He said such things were discussed openly at the high school. I looked somewhat skeptical till his sisters nodded their heads in agreement with him.

Through all of this, I have learned what a satisfying experience it is to be able to discuss all things openly with our children. Often one of the children will come and ask a personal question. As we discuss the question, others always seem to join us.

On one such occasion one of my daughters came to the kitchen table, where I was sitting, and asked me something about boys. Pretty soon her sister joined us. I noticed a few minutes later that one of the boys had brought his homework to the kitchen counter, where he was within earshot. A few minutes later another brother joined him. And after another few minutes the other brother came to the counter also. From all outward appearances they were doing their homework. However, as the girls and I continued our discussion, they interjected their opinions occasionally. Otherwise they simply listened.

Such occasions have not only brought us, as parents, closer to our children, but they have also brought our children closer together. They are open with one another and respect one another's opinions. Isn't it wonderful how, when we do the things the Lord wants us to, we're the ones who reap the rewards. Our family is much closer today because of our teaching our children about sex. Our children have more confidence in us and also in one another. It also has strengthened us as a family and welded us more firmly together.

I have witnessed the opposite effect when sex is not taught in the home. I was present once when a mother was telling a close friend about taking her twelve-year-old daughter to the doctor for a physical examination before entering seventh grade. The mother said the doctor had asked her if she had taught her daughter about her approaching puberty and the changes she could expect to occur. The mother was aghast. She certainly hadn't told her daughter, and she just couldn't do it. My heart ached for that poor girl, and I wondered what would happen to her. I kept track of her over the years, feeling certain she would be having problems. They started even before I had anticipated.

First of all, she didn't feel close to her parents. She couldn't communicate with them. (What else could be expected? The mother hadn't been able to communicate with the daughter even when a doctor advised it.) The parents couldn't handle the girl. They didn't understand her. They used a system of monetary rewards to get her to do things. They gave her tangible items when all she ever really wanted was their love, affection, and acceptance. Somehow they didn't seem to be able to reach each other. I knew that her parents loved her; I knew that she wanted to be loved. Yet the door was closed between them.

What a different situation this might have been had the mother sat down with the girl—even when she was as old as twelve—and told her she had some things to discuss with her. The mother could have told her daughter this wasn't an easy thing for her to do. The daughter would probably have been sympathetic and willing to help her mother if she knew the mother was sincerely trying. This would have opened the door between them and perhaps then it could have been kept open with each one trying. There could have evolved a good, close mother-daughter—and even a close family—relationship. Instead the mother closed the door to communication, and it has never been reopened.

The special nights I had with my Mutual class could easily be incorporated into a family situation. The father might sit down with the sons, and the mother with the daughters, or the whole family could even meet together, if desired. I used to tell my Laurels at Mutual that tonight we were going to discuss some special things. During the evening I wanted them to feel free to ask me any questions that they desired, and I would try to answer them to the best of my ability. We would open up the questions for discussion so that we could share ideas. I had previously asked the girls not to bring in friends for that night, as I wanted them to feel comfortable enough with each other to discuss their thoughts openly. I told them that I hoped no one would be embarrassed, since I wouldn't be. As I started out, most of the girls would stare at the floor, but it never took long until they all were involved and enjoying the discussion.

I usually started the evening out by talking about the attraction a girl feels toward a boy and vice versa. I told them these are natural physical tendencies, and they are ordained of God. The main purpose for these feelings is so that children will be born into the world. God has set rules, however, regarding these feelings. To break these rules brings about very serious consequences. Then I would go into the laws of chastity, discussing exactly what each law means and what the punishment is for breaking it. I explained such terms as necking and petting and the serious consequences involved, what these actions can easily lead to, and why. I explained to the girls the seriousness of sitting in a parked car with a boy, and advised them never to do it. I explained the difference between how a girl gets "turned on" and how a boy does. I explained how much more serious it could be for a girl if she got "turned on"—how easily she could reach the point of no return. I explained the symptoms of such a condition and what to do if it ever happened to them. We discussed what a beautiful spiritual experience making love is when done within the sanctity of marriage. We also discussed the heartache, the anguish, and the torment of mind that follow if such things are participated in outside of wedlock. We discussed repentance, but emphasized that it is a hard climb back up a very narrow, steep path.

The pattern of each special night evolved on its own as the girls participated. The direction we went depended a lot on the type and amount of questions they asked. Sometimes the night was extended for another class period. At the conclusion I always encouraged the girls to go home and pray about the things we had discussed. I asked them to make a special effort to discuss these things with their parents or at least with their mothers. I also told them to be sure that when they became mothers they taught and trained their own children along these lines. I bore my testimony and cautioned them to take the steps we had outlined during the class to keep themselves pure and holy before the Lord, to seek the Lord's help in finding a proper mate, and to prepare for a temple marriage and never be satisfied with anything less.

This special night can be adapted well to a family home evening. It can give parents an opportunity to discuss with their children these important principles that should be taught in the home. What a very close feeling can be shared by all during such an evening! It can be one evening the children will long remember and one they will hold dear to their hearts.

Chapter 13

The Dating Game

Another important subject that parents should discuss freely with their children is dating. When I was growing up the Church hadn't set a standard age for dating. As a result I was allowed to date very early, and I had some experiences that I was too young and immature to handle.

I am one person who is most grateful the Church has taken a stand on dating and has advised us we shouldn't date before we're sixteen. To some this seems harsh, I know. However, if parents will teach their children from the time they're small about dating—what it is, when it will be allowed, and what will be expected of them—many of their problems will be alleviated.

From Webster we learn that a date is an appointment with a specified person. I take this to mean that when a boy invites a girl to do something with him on a certain occasion, it is a date. It might be a drive in the country, a picnic at the park, going to a ballgame, seeing a movie, or going to dinner or to a dance. When the Church specifies sixteen as the age to date, I take it to mean sixteen in the same way that age eight is the age to be baptized. When a child reaches eight years of age, the Lord feels he has reached an age when he can be accountable for his own sins. When he reaches sixteen, he has reached an age when he can be responsible enough to date.

One day my fifteen-year-old son wanted to go on a picnic with a girl he liked and another couple. I reminded him that he was not yet sixteen. He said they wouldn't be alone, as the other couple would be with them. Besides, the girls were already fixing the lunch. I told him I didn't approve.

He became a little upset with me and said I didn't trust him. I told him it had nothing to do with trust. I reminded him I had taught him since he was a tiny boy that in our home one wouldn't be allowed to date before age sixteen. He said that was only three months away. I told him I realized that, but the Brethren hadn't said three months before one is sixteen. They had said sixteen. He again accused me of not trusting him and of feeling that he would do something wrong.

I looked him straight in the eye and told him I *knew* he wouldn't do anything wrong. It was merely a matter of principle. He went out of the room, discussed it with his friend, and then came back. He wanted to know what he could do to make it acceptable. I told him to get some more young people to go along and make it a group affair instead of a date affair.

He worked on his brother for a while, trying to get him to go along. Failing in this attempt, he finally succeeded in coaxing two other boys to go. I gave my approval, and they went.

What my son failed to realize was that he really had his own freedom. Had he just said, "I'm going on a picnic with —— and another couple," I would have voiced my disapproval but wouldn't have prevented his going. But perhaps because of all our instruction on dating, he respected our wishes and sought our approval. This was the only occasion in several months when he asked permission to go somewhere. Consistent with our policy of cutting the apron strings at age fourteen, it had been his practice merely to inform us of his intended activities. I admired him because he had respect for our teachings and my feelings in this matter. He could have done it without my approval, but he chose not to go against my wishes.

Early dating can lead to problems. One girl I knew started dating when she was twelve, as did many of her friends. By the time she was thirteen, simple dating wasn't enough fun, so she started going steady. As if that weren't bad enough by itself, she went with someone much older than she, a young man who had already been married and divorced. By the time she was almost fourteen, boys near her own age had no appeal for her. She was always interested in the much older ones. At the rate she was going, it was a miracle she wasn't married by the time she reached sixteen—before she'd really had time to mature, make good decisions, and really have fun in life.

So many young people have asked me what is really wrong with dating before one is sixteen. First of all, I point out that it is wrong because the Brethren have said not to do it. I then quote D&C 1:38: "Whether by mine own voice or by the voice of my servants, it is the same."

Second, I explain that perhaps the Lord is trying them to see if they will be obedient. I tell them the story of King Saul (1 Samuel 15), who was told by the prophet Samuel to destroy all the Amalekites (including men, women, and children), all their belongings, and all their animals. "But Saul and the people spared Agag, and the best of the sheep, and of the oxen, and of the fatlings, and the lambs, and all that was good, and would not utterly destroy them." The Lord told Samuel what had happened, and Samuel went to Saul. Saul told Samuel that he had carried out the Lord's command. And then Samuel said, "What meaneth then this bleating of the sheep in mine ears, and the lowing of the oxen which I hear?" Saul told Samuel that the best of the sheep and oxen had been spared to offer as a sacrifice unto the Lord. Then Samuel said to Saul: "Hath the Lord as great delight in burnt offerings and sacrifices as in obeying the voice of the Lord? Behold, to obey is better than sacrifice, and to hearken than the fat of rams." Saul was told that because of his disobedience, his kingdom would be taken from him and given to another. I then explain to the youth that they too may lose their kingdoms if they choose to be disobedient.

Third, I point out that if a person starts dating too early, he may become involved in becoming too serious before he is mature enough to make wise decisions. President Spencer W. Kimball has said: "Dating in the earlier teen-age years leads to early steady dating with its multiplicity of dangers and problems, and frequently to early and disappointing marriage. This too-young dating is not uncommon and is often done with parental approval. Yet it is near criminal to subject a tender child to the temptations of maturity. Early marriages, which are almost certain of failure, are usually the result of steady, early dating, whereas a proper preparation for marriage is a well-timed courtship." (*The Miracle of Forgiveness,* Bookcraft, 1969, p. 223.)

President Kimball goes on to tell about a girl who had been allowed to date before she was sixteen and now had a problem. As her parents sat there in his office he thought, "Mother, where were you when she was dating steady at fourteen? Were you off to work or were you just asleep? Or were you trying to have another young romance for yourself, by proxy? Where were you when your little girl started dating?" (*The Miracle of Forgiveness,* p. 223.)

I ask them how long they can date before they want to go steady. How long—if at all—can they go steady before they start kissing? How long can they go on kissing before they start getting serious? Then I explain that this process cheats them of building good friendships from which true love evolves.

Teaching our children the hows and whys of the dating process is very important. One thing I have taught my children is that marriage should grow out of a well-established friendship.

I use a scale of one through ten, as follows:

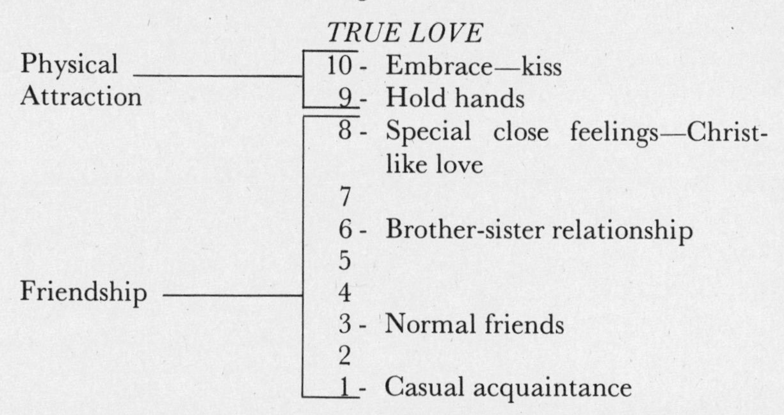

I explain that on this scale of one through ten, numbers one through eight should be pure friendship. This kind of friendship builds up from a casual acquaintance at level one to what we normally call friends somewhere around level three. Then the friendship builds to where one knows the person quite well, like a brother or sister, at level five to six. Somewhere between six and eight one reaches the stage where he has a very special close feeling for this person. This is similar to the feelings we have for someone we really admire, such as a church official or a teacher. It's a genuine respect mingled with a great admiration that grows into a Christlike quality of love.

When a couple have established this type of friendship, then they have laid a proper foundation and are ready to move on to levels nine and ten. This is where they begin to hold hands, embrace each other, and finally, at level ten, kiss each other. How beautiful a relationship would be if a couple could truly go through all the levels to level ten before they kissed. This would be the level of true love and engagement.

Contrast this with couples who start kissing after the second or third date. Too often this leads to a pattern of kissing, and the persons involved fail to get to know each other well. What they have done is skipped from level one to level ten without going through the other levels. They get involved in physical attraction and fail to know each other well enough to establish a firm, marriageable relationship. This is the difference between true love and infatuation. Infatuation is a physical attraction that involves physical pleasure. True love is a spiritual attraction that involves the spirit and brings true joy.

Couples who get married with a relationship based on infatuation have a greater chance of ending up getting a divorce. Often they don't have anything strong enough on which to build a lasting relationship. Many couples go farther up the scale. They work up to level three or four and then skip up to level nine or ten. They learn to know each other as normal friends and then get involved in physical attraction. Couples who get married with only this much of a friendship relationship have many serious problems. They have to go on and try to build up through levels four, five, six, seven, and eight after they are married, and that's a difficult process. Marriage brings enough problems without a couple's having to backtrack and build a relationship that should have been established before marriage. Many such marriages eventually end up in divorce, some many years later, even after the children are gone. Children tend to hold this type of marriage together, but after they are gone, it becomes too difficult at that age for the couple to try to reach levels four, five, six, and seven. It's amazing that couples can live together for years and yet fail to get to know each other well enough to establish a level seven relationship.

Many couples who have skipped from level three to level eight do backtrack and make successful marriages. Often it is because they both have testimonies of the gospel. This holds their marriage together till they reach level seven, where their friendship relationship has a strong enough base to take over. Of course, couples with strong testimonies will always work out their problems, for they realize there is no other alternative.

We need to teach our children the hazards of shortcuts in the dating process and the problems they create in a marriage relationship. Then we need to help them live with the smarter system, for those who believe in and try to practice this one-to-ten relationship may experience a lot of frustration generated by their peers.

My son, at age fifteen, knew a girl in whom he was quite interested. He had developed a friendship relationship with her through school classes and Saturday night stake dances they both attended. They didn't date. At the dances other boys and girls would try to get them to hold hands. My son wouldn't do it, and yet it was frustrating to him to always have his friends nagging him about it. I explained the levels to him and told him to hold his ground. It would pay dividends in the long run.

We discussed the situation several times. He was willing to wait till he had worked up through the levels properly. I explained how if nothing ever came from this relationship, he would never have to have any regrets. He and the girl could always be the best of friends. This was an opportune time to explain how kissing can truly be a spiritual experience. If physical attraction alone is present, then a kiss merely produces physical pleasure. However, if the proper foundation has been laid by going through levels one through nine, then when one kisses someone at level ten, it is a spiritual union. This is because of the very special deep feelings of true love that have been established. A spirit-to-spirit relationship is involved, creating a spiritual experience that produces true joy.

After I explained this to my son, he was more willing to wait, but it is hard for some youths to accept this theory. Perhaps it is because they haven't developed to a high enough spiritual level to accept it. Perhaps it's like trying to teach them calculus before they've had basic math. I have found that those who have grown to a proper spiritual level can and will accept this theory. I also feel that children who have been raised from the beginning with this type of instruction don't have much difficulty accepting it either.

Another problem young people in the Church run into occasionally is whether they should accept a date from a nonmember. I have always been very strict where this is concerned, and have advised my children not to date nonmembers because one marries the people he dates.

I have heard many arguments for and against this concept, but President Kimball has pointed out the importance of proper dating: "Clearly, right marriage begins with right dating. A person generally marries someone from among those with whom he associates, with whom he goes to school, with whom he goes to church, with whom he socializes. Therefore, this warning comes with great emphasis. Do not take the chance of dating nonmembers, or members who are untrained and faithless. A girl may say, 'Oh, I do not intend to marry this person. It is just a "fun" date.' But one cannot afford to take a chance on falling in love with someone who may never accept the gospel. True, a small percentage have finally been baptized after marrying Church members. Some good women and some good men have joined the Church after the mixed marriage and have remained devout and active. We are proud of them and grateful for them. They are our blessed *minority.* Others who did not join the Church were still kind and considerate and cooperative and permitted the member spouse to worship and serve according to the Church patterns. But the *majority* did not join the Church and, as indicated earlier, friction, frustration and divorce marked a great many of their marriages." (*The Miracle of Forgiveness,* pp. 241-42. Italics added.)

My parents never told me when to be home from a date. But when I came home later than they thought I should, I was in trouble. Because of this I was determined to set a time limit for my children. I read a story when they were quite young telling how one set of parents solved this problem. When one of their children went on a date, the parents told him when they expected him home. They set an alarm clock for the appointed hour. If the child arrived home on time, he could turn off the alarm and everyone was happy. If he didn't arrive home on time, the alarm went off and woke up the parents. Then they weren't so happy.

I thought this a good idea to keep in reserve to use with my children when they reached the dating age. However, I have found it unnecessary to use such a system with them. They have been totally trustworthy and have not given me any cause for concern.

Another important concept for young people to be familiar with is how to treat each other with respect. We have tried to teach our children that it is proper for boys to open doors for girls—doors to cars, doors to houses, and doors to buildings. A girl should wait in the car while the boy walks around and lets her out. She should step aside so he can open the door to a building for her.

When I was young and dating, I thought boys did such nice things for girls only while they were dating. After I was married I assumed I would now be expected to open the car door myself. The first time I tried it, my husband was quick to inform me that that was one thing he always expected to do for me. He asked me in the future to please wait till he could open the door for me. I was surprised but also delighted. After twenty-one years of marriage, he is still opening doors for me. What a perfect example for his sons to follow (and his daughters to expect)!

Another courtesy my husband shows me is that he always walks on the outside when we are walking down a street. If we cross a street, putting him on the inside, he crosses behind me so he is on the outside again. He puts his arm out for me to hold onto. He takes my elbow as I step off a curb. All these things he continues to do though we have been married many years. Example is the best teacher, so if a father coaches his sons in this regard and also sets the example, it will be much easier for the son to react positively.

It is a matter of good manners for a man to stand when a woman walks into the room or when being introduced. A man also offers a woman his seat if there are no vacant ones in the room. The world would have us disregard such courtesies in its attempt to bring women to a level equal with men. However, boys in the Church should still be schooled in the old-fashioned respect extended to women.

Children should be taught well the fundamentals of chastity and virtue. They should be warned about danger signs and pitfalls. Praying with a youth before he goes on a date will help him remember the standards he is expected to keep. It sets the stage for having the Lord's presence with youth while they're dating. I would advise young people to avoid circumstances and areas that might lead them into difficult situations. For example, it is much safer to do things with a group or to double date than to be alone as a couple. Spending a great deal of time together alone isn't the safest thing; it's better to have at least one other couple go along. The couple can still get better acquainted with each other, but under more secure circumstances.

Going to the movies or watching television can be entertaining, but these don't do much to help a couple get to know one another well. I'm not saying they should never do such things, but their friendship level will develop faster if they include activities in which they can be more involved, activities that help them to communicate with each other. Playing games, ice skating, and going to sporting events, dances, and other such activities where they don't have to be quiet are more conducive to getting to know each other.

Another consideration for a girl in dating is the boy's finances. A couple can do many things that take little money or none at all. Sometimes a boy would date a girl more often if he could afford it. She might suggest doing some things that don't cost anything, so he will realize that she can be satisfied just being in his company without having to have expensive entertainment. After a date, when a boy suggests going out for something to eat, a girl might offer to prepare something at her house. This gives the boy a way out if he desires, and lets the girl help share in the expense of the date. Parents might help out in this area by having cookies and ice cream, popcorn, or waffle fixings available so the girl can extend such an offer. The boy can always insist on eating out if he can easily afford it and would rather.

Following are some things I have learned about dating from teaching teenage boys and girls that might be helpful:

A boy wants to date a girl who is interested in what he is doing. If he is interested in athletics, she should direct the conversation toward this subject. She should follow the events so she has some idea of what is going on in his field.

A girl should never be moody. She should put aside her feelings and try to be pleasant. There are always exceptions, of course; and if there is really something bothering her, perhaps she could discuss it with the boy. He might be flattered to have her display this confidence in him.

A girl shouldn't play tricks on a boy that put him in an embarrassing situation.

A girl shouldn't keep a boy waiting when he comes to pick her up. He doesn't want to sit and talk with her parents for long periods of time—he didn't make the date with them.

A girl should treat her family with respect—especially her brothers and sisters.

A girl shouldn't sit against the opposite car door as if she's afraid of her date, but she shouldn't be on his lap either.

A boy should never honk for a girl.

A boy shouldn't call up and ask for a date and then ask what the girl wants to do. How does she know what he wants to spend or what he might have in mind? He should make some suggestions when he asks for the date. She, on the other hand, shouldn't say that she doesn't care—they can do whatever he wants to do. If she doesn't care, why should he even bother to take her out?

A girl should tell a boy what time she is expected to be home. He doesn't want her parents angry with him.

Girls and boys should speak respectfully to one another. Being sarcastic is in very poor taste, and it could easily offend one or the other though they might be quick to cover up and act to the contrary.

Girls want to be remembered on special occasions. Boys appreciate it too, but are not as emotional about it. Boys appreciate receiving cookies or candy on Valentine's Day, not just a card. They appreciate it when girls recognize their birthday. Girls expect boys to remember every special occasion and are usually secretly hurt if they don't.

Girls appreciate little touching surprises. On the Mother's Day before our marriage, my husband sent me a corsage and a beautiful, expressive note by way of the florist. I was very touched although a little dismayed that he had spent money he could ill afford. On our first wedding anniversary, I received a special surprise. He was in college and working part-time. I was working also and badly needed a new pair of shoes, but our finances were very limited. I had been able to save enough money out of my meager grocery allowance to buy material to make him a shirt. I knew he had no way of getting extra money, so I really didn't expect a present. It was Saturday, so I was home that day while he was at work. When I went out to get the mail, I found an envelope addressed to me in his handwriting. Inside was a lovely card. On it he expressed to me in beautiful language how much our first year together had meant. Also tucked inside was a five-dollar bill with a note telling me to go buy some new shoes. I sat out on our front porch and sobbed openly. He could have just given me the five dollars or even left a card at the house. But he planned the gift-giving out and made it very special.

Girls and boys both in this day and age need to be particularly careful with how they view womanhood. Satan is out working very hard, gathering his forces and combining his efforts to wage one final battle before the millennium begins. He is not stupid either. He held a high place in our premortal life as Lucifer, son of the morning. He had the privilege of presenting an alternate plan for our earthly existence. He had intelligence, but he was not wise. Now he is using this master intelligence to try to conquer mankind and thus frustrate the plans of God.

How is Satan using his intelligence in our day? He is so cunning one almost has to look twice to recognize the craftiness of his plans. He is attacking the high standard of womanhood through government and women's groups. Why is he doing that? What effect will it really have? Well, it can only undermine the whole human race!

It used to be that some men (speaking of the world in general, not the Church) might engage in somewhat raw conversation using crude language, but if a woman were to walk into the area where this was going on, such language would cease. Women used to be regarded as having higher standards, but now many women have insisted upon bringing themselves down to the level of men. Many men no longer cease crude language when a woman enters. They no longer look upon her as a "lady," but as an equal. She is included in their vulgarities and often takes an active part.

How does this lowering of standards in women affect the whole human race? The General Authorities often mention a man's achievements and credit them to a good woman behind him—a good wife or mother or both. (See "The Women of God," by Neal A. Maxwell, *Ensign,* May 1978, pp. 10-11.) President Spencer W. Kimball has told of his call to the Council of the Twelve and of how very inadequate he felt. His lovely wife, Camilla, supported him and helped him. When he cried and said he couldn't do it, she was there to encourage him and say, "You can do it, you can do it." (*Ensign,* May 1978, p. 11.) I also recall reading about President Kimball's telling missionaries that every man should marry a woman who was better than he was and who would pull him up to her level. "Marry her in the temple and be sure she is better than you are. I would never be in the Council of the Twelve today if I had married some of the girls that I have known. Sister Kimball kept me growing and never let me be satisfied with mediocrity." (*Spencer W. Kimball,* Bookcraft, 1977, p. 317.) Women influence both their husbands and their children. If Satan can undermine the high standards of womanhood, he will lower the standards of the entire human race. If he can get women on his side, he will have all the army he needs. His ways are indeed cunning and crafty. We have to be alert to recognize what he is trying to do.

Looking at it from the other side, womanhood can be very fulfilling—not at all the picture Satan is trying to paint. Women have the great privilege of being co-creators with God. They have the opportunity of preparing mortal tabernacles for God's spirit children. While a mother is carrying a child within her, she has an opportunity to have a special close feeling to God. She realizes the many things that could go wrong with this unborn child. She has to rely on God for the child's health and welfare and the knowledge she needs to properly care for herself during this period.

After what seems like forever, the birth process begins. Again, the mother feels a real closeness to God and a dependence upon him. After the baby is born, she has the privilege of caring for someone who has come from the presence of God. What could this spirit tell her if only he could speak?

When a woman thinks about the great opportunity that a mother has, how could she ever sacrifice it and fall prey to the worldly philosophies that would have her limit the number of children she has—or even not have children at all?

The joys and satisfaction that can come to a mother are almost indescribable. Picture, if you will, an eighteen-year-old boy walking to the pulpit to bear his testimony. He begins and then his voice breaks, and he cries silently without being able to talk for a few moments. Finally he stands firm and erect and bears witness of his great love for the Lord. The joy I felt as my son walked down from the stand that day was similar to the feelings I had one Christmas morning as I read the card from my daughter containing this message:

"Mother, today I decided to thank everyone for the gifts they have shared with me. I saved you for last. I could write a book on the gifts you have given me. It's only right that a mother would give the most. I could thank you for teaching me to sew, to cook, to clean house, and I do thank you for those lessons. But today, Mother, I want to thank you for the lessons you have taught that mean the very most. You know how the scripture goes—Joseph Smith has done more, save Jesus Christ, for our salvation than any man. Well, next to those two, Mother, is you! You have taught me through the Spirit that Jesus Christ lives. I could write poetry, beautiful words—but could it mean more than just this: because of your influence on my life, Jesus is a real person to me. Because of you I know he lives. In D&C 18:15-16 it says your joy will be great if you bring one soul unto Christ. Mother, I hope your joy is full—because of you, mine is. Mother, I know He lives! I love Him. I love you."

To all my teenage friends—and youth everywhere—I would say: Never sell yourself short, for the Lord has great blessings in store for you. Satan would have you believe otherwise and will do all in his power to sell you on his way of life. But he will not support you in the end, and your losses will be more than your soul will want to endure. Date wisely, and listen to your parents' advice. After all, they've been teenagers too!

Chapter 14

The Mark of Mormonism

Teenagers, despite what some people may think, are not looking for trouble. They are looking for happiness—for acceptance. Without a parent's guiding influence and love, they may never find the right road. I have seen many teenagers waste away a good part of their lives earnestly seeking in the wrong direction. They go from job to job, from town to town, from friend to friend, from cigarettes to alcohol to drugs, seeking happiness but finding only fleeting pleasure. Most often teenagers raised in the Church would find what they're seeking in their own homes if they knew how to go about it. What they're really seeking, whether they know it or not, is the spiritual experience that comes from knowing that the gospel is true and that God does live and he loves them.

Teenagers really want and need spiritual highs, but they're being misguided by the forces of evil. They're being led to seek these highs through drugs, drinks, and immorality. Momentarily they may feel they have succeeded, but how hard it is to reclaim them from the deep pits they are digging for themselves.

How much easier it is for youth if they are prevented from ever falling into such pits. Parents need to use some preventive gospel therapy. They need to teach their children to have faith in the Lord, to repent of their wrongdoings, to seek for the guiding influence of the Holy Ghost, and above all to keep the commandments. Basic principles? Yes. But these fundamentals will lead them to the spiritual high they are seeking—a testimony. We must start when they are little and teach them to pray to be worthy to go on missions and to get married in the temple. We must teach them to pray for protection from the evils of the world, such as drugs, alcohol, and tobacco. When our youngest was four years old I taught her to pray that she would get married in the temple and never take alcohol or tobacco or drugs.

After several weeks of praying this way, one night she looked up at me and asked what drugs were. Maybe the children won't know exactly what they're praying about at first, but the ideas will become a part of their lives.

When the children are older and we don't listen to their private prayers anymore, we can still use family prayer to keep the thought constantly before them. We can pray for their welfare where they can hear us. We can use family prayer as a teaching device. This will serve a dual purpose: We will enlist the Lord's help in caring for and protecting our children, and it will also let them know that we are genuinely concerned about them and care what happens to them. It will help serve as a protective shield in case they are tempted to go wrong. And, basically, it will remind them that their parents expect the best from them.

Sometimes we may be perfectly willing to listen and to give time to our teenager, but somehow we still fail to communicate properly. Sometimes children go through stages when we may try everything we know how to do and still fail to reach them. We mustn't give up! Perhaps they have a teacher at school or church or even a neighbor that they seem to enjoy, someone whose help we could enlist. We shouldn't be afraid to seek help from others—just because they can reach our teenager when we can't doesn't mean we have failed. We fail if we have help available and don't use it.

When our son reached twelve, he seemed to hit a phase when nothing we said or did had much influence on him. I was really concerned. When I finally accepted the fact that I was no longer reaching him, I knew I had to do something. I had sensed that he felt close to his Scoutmaster and also his deacons quorum adviser, so I approached both of these men and expressed my concerns regarding some of my son's attitudes. I asked for their help. They were both very dedicated men and were glad to help in any way they could. I noted after our conference the special interest they each took in my son. They made it a point to speak to him at church meetings and to call and talk to him occasionally during the week. He was also their paper boy, so their paths crossed quite often. The point is, if we are having difficulty reaching our children, and can see that help is needed, we shouldn't be afraid to ask. These spirits entrusted to our care are so very important that we should never hesitate in doing things that will be for their benefit.

Another of our sons is quite shy. As a little boy, he would run and hide behind the living room door whenever someone came to visit. If anyone spoke directly to him or asked him a question, he would be so scared that he would almost cry. Each new event in his life seemed to be a trial. He has a natural ability for sports, but I couldn't get him to even try out for a team.

Finally one day I decided to talk to the coach of the track team about our son. The coach had a way with boys and really understood the situation. He didn't ask our son if he wanted to be on the track team. When the occasion was right he simply pointed his finger at him and said, "You are going to be on the track team. Be at the next practice." I didn't hear about this from this son, but his brother was quick to inform me. I asked if our son had said he would be there. His brother said he had just grinned. However, he showed up for practice. As it worked out, running wasn't the thing he was really interested in, but that year on the track team did a world of good for him. He learned how to associate with other boys and really felt a part of the group. When we went to the finals where his older brother was running, he didn't sit with us. As soon as we got to the bleachers he looked for the rest of the boys on the track team and went to sit with them. I was delighted because he was not only accepted by the group, but he also took the initiative to be a part of them. Now he is able to make his own way. I'm sure that if we seek for help with the problems that arise with our children, we will be guided to satisfactory solutions. Whatever the crisis, we simply must not give up!

One of the most important things we can do to help our teenagers is to pray for them. A Sunday School teacher once told of how his mother prayed for him and the influence it had had on him. He had an appointment to apply for a job one morning and left the house early after saying goodbye to his mother. After a few minutes out on the road he realized he had forgotten something, so he turned around and returned to the house. When he entered he heard his mother speaking. Not wishing to disturb her, he moved about noiselessly. As he went past her room he saw her on her knees—the person to whom she had been talking had been her Heavenly Father. He heard her pleading with the Lord to be with her son that morning—to guide him in making a proper decision regarding the job offer. "Let him be guided to do what will be best for him," she asked.

His mother's prayer had made such a deep impression on him that years later he related this special incident to other people. The influence a parent has should never be underestimated.

Take the example of Alma the younger in the Book of Mormon. He, along with the four sons of Mosiah, had gone about preaching against the church. They had been reared by good parents, but somehow they were misguided in their beliefs. They were a great hindrance to the building up of the kingdom of God in their day. One day an angel appeared to them and told them that what they were doing was wrong. He told Alma the younger that he had come in answer to the prayers of the boy's father. Alma became one of the outstanding prophets in the Book of Mormon and gave the rest of his life in service to God and his fellowmen. He changed from a sinful man to a very righteous man. And how was the miracle accomplished? Because his father and other members of the Church had faith enough that they wouldn't give up. (See Mosiah 27.)

What an outstanding example this is for us! If our children should stray, we must never give up. We must have the courage and trust that Alma the elder displayed. No matter how trying the circumstances or how hopeless the situation may seem to be, we can always have hope. If we are living righteous lives ourselves, then we can seek for God's help and can have the faith that he will aid us in reaching our children.

The responsibility still rests on us, however. We must ask for God's help in such trying circumstances, and he will not abandon us. But children may ignore the influence of the Lord, much as Laman and Lemuel did. The Lord sent an angel to them also (1 Nephi 3:29), and gave them several opportunities to get back on the right path, but they chose to ignore all the pricks of conscience till they had reached the point where they could no longer feel the Spirit. (1 Nephi 17:45.) They cut themselves off from the Lord. Father Lehi went to his grave worrying over these wayward sons; his grief was immense. (2 Nephi 1.) But he wasn't alone, for God knows the grief of losing children through rebellion. He lost one-third of his spirit children before this life began.

We are never alone in our suffering. Our Father in heaven will seek to soften the hearts of our wayward children so they can see the errors of their ways, but we must have unending faith and courage. We must fast and pray often for these special spirits who have momentarily gone astray. Above all, we must never lose hope. We must never give up, for nothing is really lost until we quit trying.

Something we as parents often fail to realize is that youth don't have the testimonies we do. They are young and inexperienced. They are still learning and growing. They need a great deal of love, understanding, and gentle persuasion during this unsteady period of their lives. We can't expect them to feel the same toward gospel standards and principles as we do.

When our oldest daughter hit the teenage era, miniskirts were the rage. I was teaching Laurels at the time and had a couple of lessons each year on modesty. I felt very strongly that I couldn't go and talk to these girls about how they should wear their dresses if my own girls weren't doing as I advised. I explained this to my daughters. At first it wasn't a problem, but many of the girls teased my daughter about her dress lengths. She asked me if I wouldn't make her skirts shorter. I explained to her why she needed to wear them where I made them. I wasn't actually listening to what she was saying: she was really telling me it was hard to be different from all the other girls. Perhaps if I had understood, she wouldn't have objected. Well, she grew five inches in one year, and her dresses got shorter fast, but I was determined, so I made her new dresses. She tried them on before I hemmed them and was dismayed at their length. She asked how long I was going to make them; I told her to the knee. I could see how distressed she was, but I was determined to live the letter of the law—completely forgetting that people are more important.

One Saturday she sat on the desk in the kitchen while I was working and brought up the topic of dress lengths again. I tried reasoning with her, but again I wasn't listening. Finally in exasperation I took a dollar bill out of my wallet and put it in her hand. I told her to go buy a package of cigarettes and smoke them. She gave the bill back to me, as I had expected, and said she would not. Then I explained that in my estimation wearing miniskirts was no different than smoking a package of cigarettes. Either way you were breaking a law. She went out of the room silently. I assumed I had won the battle.

Later, my husband sat me down and did some serious talking to me. He told me I may have won the battle, but if I kept going in the same direction I might lose the war. He told me I could force our daughter right out of the Church.

What insight, what perception he had. I had virtually closed the door to communication with her. I had not been willing to really listen and understand.

I went to this daughter and told her that thereafter when I sewed for her I would hem the dresses according to church standards. If she wanted them shorter, she would have to re-hem them. I wouldn't stop her, but neither would I help her violate a standard.

What a lot I had to learn, and most of it seemed to come through hard knocks to our oldest child. I sometimes wonder how she ever managed to keep existing while I learned. I seemed to be totally oblivious of God's way of teaching: line upon line, and precept upon precept.

When we aren't always able to achieve as the Lord would have us do, does he get upset with us and become intolerant? No. He keeps on trying. I feel sure that he expects us to show this same tolerance and understanding with our children. God doesn't demand of us, and we shouldn't demand of our children. Even though they are teenagers, many are still like babes in arms as far as their spiritual growth and understanding are concerned. Their testimonies are a little shaky at this point in their lives. Whether their foundation becomes strong and sure is often entirely dependent upon us, their parents.

After I had gone through this period of learning with our oldest daughter, I was much wiser. I really learned that we parents have to spoon-feed teenagers spiritually a dose at a time. When they have received a sufficient portion, they will take over and start feeding themselves. Until they reach that point, we must guard cautiously against the worldly termites that would come in and invade and tear down from within the structure we are so patiently trying to build.

One of my neighbors asked advice concerning her sixteen-year-old son's hair length. He was a good boy and had never given his parents much cause for concern. Long hair for boys was in vogue; it was something new, and he wanted to try it. His mother was upset because of the image associated with long hair. She asked me what to do. I reminded her that he was a good boy, and suggested that she not overreact. It was most likely a phase that he would soon outgrow if she didn't reinforce the behavior by her obvious objections to it. I told her to tell him how she felt about it but to let him make up his own mind. Her son did let his hair grow, but not for long. He found out that it wasn't very cool in the summer, and soon had it cut.

One of my own sons wanted to lengthen his hairstyle. He had a more difficult time achieving exactly what he wanted because his mother was his barber. But I asked his advice several times during the haircut, and when I was through he seemed to be satisfied. His hair was longer than I liked it, but it was still above his shirt collar and cut over his ears. The problem was that to me he looked as if he was due for a haircut. Sure enough, about two weeks later he was back for another cut. He somewhat sheepishly asked me to cut his hair as I had been doing before. He found out he really liked his appearance better when it was shorter. I am sure his actions would have been defiant had I insisted on having my way with his hair. In reality I would have been forcing.

I really don't believe that forcing is God's way. We can always dish out stronger dosages when our children are spiritually mature enough to handle them. But we wouldn't try to feed adult aspirin or medicine to a small child: what would be helpful to the adult could be lethal to the child. And so it is with spirituality—it must be administered according to what the person's tolerance level is. Otherwise we might be guilty of spiritually poisoning our children.

Sometimes parents have problems reaching teenagers because of the gravitational pull in opposite directions. Both children and parents are influenced by their peers, and there is a certain amount of pressure on both. Peer pressure among teenagers can have a tremendous pull away from parental guidance and influence. Parents too receive a certain amount of peer pressure, and it may not always be in the best interest of the children.

For instance, sometimes a bishop or some other church leader has a child who is somewhat rebellious, and right away some people put labels on the child and the parent. How often have you heard, "Well, he's the bishop's son. He should know better." Many people are outspoken and say exactly what they think, which usually tends to push parent and child further apart. The amazing thing is that such people fail to realize that they have a responsibility toward the child too. It would be so much more beneficial if, instead of judging the child, they would spend that time trying to fellowship him. Some of these adults might easily end up having more persuasive power over a wayward teenager than his own peers have. The result could easily be another soul saved.

Another way parents are influenced by their peers is in the way they act toward their children when other adults are present. Too often a parent will be extremely harsh with a child in the presence of another adult, when the parent would not generally react that way. The opposite can also be true: a parent who usually disciplines well might beg or bribe a child while in the presence of another adult. Parents may put too much emphasis on what they believe another adult is thinking, instead of doing what is best for their child.

For example, if our small child isn't willing to share something of his own accord, I don't feel he should be forced. His possessions are his. They are part of his world—part of his security. If we force him to give them to someone else before he's ready, it may tend to make him selfish. We should let him have his possessions long enough to know that they are truly his. We should talk to him about sharing, and whenever he does share, we should praise his action a lot. When he doesn't choose to share, we mustn't shame him or put emphasis on negative behavior. When the parents of his friends are over, we shouldn't insist he share if he doesn't want to. I know it may be embarrassing. Other adults may label us and point accusing fingers, but who is more important—them or our child? Remember, nothing reinforces misbehavior so much as criticism of that behavior. We must try to look for positive actions and praise them.

I sincerely believe that parents have to realize that their children are more important than other people. We should not be influenced by what others might think where our children are concerned—we should do what we feel is best for them on all occasions. Otherwise, their peers and our peers are having a tug-of-war. The end result is that parent and child are pulled further and further apart.

How would it affect you if someone in authority over you in a church position came to you and delivered an ultimatum about something he expected you to do? Perhaps I am different from many people, but I think it would tend to raise my blood pressure. I might be perfectly willing to do what had been assigned me, but the manner in which the request was delivered might totally turn me off.

I think our children are often affected in this same manner by the way we approach them. Too often our demands tend to cause their blood pressure to rise. It may be that they are really not totally against doing what we are demanding, but our approach is negative, and it brings a negative response from them. Then we have created a crisis.

How much better it would be if we could always be Christlike in our approach to our children. They may be completely against what we are suggesting, but if we are kind, gentle, and understanding, we can usually have much more influence upon them. We weaken their resistance when we use a more spiritual approach. We seem to reach beyond the rough exterior, and the spirit within tends to be more cooperative.

If we have been demanding and authoritarian, the first time we use a humble, positive approach our child may be on the defensive. He may view this as a new tactic we are using in the war we have been waging against him. It may take several such approaches before he will weaken his fortifications and be willing to take a chance at a truce. He may be cautious for a long time and not be completely willing to put his trust in us. We mustn't give up. Remember, a thousand-mile journey begins with the first step. Each step forward takes us that much closer to reaching our goal. Above all, once we have begun such a journey, we must never resort to old tactics, or we may never again be able to break through our child's well-built barriers.

Sometimes there will be occasions when we cannot lower our standards. We simply cannot give in to our child, as it would be extremely detrimental to his welfare. Just as we would not let a small child touch a hot stove because of the injury he would sustain, so we cannot let a teenager walk down dangerous or forbidden paths because of the spiritual burn he might receive. On these occasions, approach is all-important. If we become authoritarian and demanding we must be prepared for that child to walk out on us—perhaps permanently. We need to be cautious—not timid—as we tell him that what he wants simply cannot be. Remember, his eternal welfare may well depend on how well we handle such situations. At best teenagers are walking through difficult and trying times. They need all the help and understanding we can give.

A friend once approached me about one of her children who was causing her some concern. She told me of several escapades she'd had with this son. He wasn't a teenager yet, but always seemed to be causing trouble. The boy was a middle child in a large family. I asked her if she could read between the lines and see what he really was telling her. She thought for a moment and said he needed attention. I agreed. But she said that with such a large family she just couldn't spend that much time with one child. I didn't quite have the nerve to tell her what I wanted to say.

We're always having emergencies with children. If a child comes in bleeding severely, we drop everything and try to stop the bleeding. If a child comes in with a broken bone, we drop everything and rush him to the doctor. Likewise, when a child is bleeding emotionally, we need to drop everything and handle the crisis and stop the bleeding. Otherwise, he may sustain a severe internal injury.

One way to help develop a better relationship with a child is to have respect for his possessions. A parent should never take or use anything of the child's without first obtaining his permission. After all, we don't appreciate their using our things without asking.

Some time ago I was gathering all my materials together for a stake spiritual living lesson. I put them near the front door where they'd be handy. I didn't want to forget anything, so I tried to have everything for my evening meeting organized and together early in the afternoon. I needed a picture of the Savior for my lesson, so I got one we had bought for my youngest daughter and set it out near my things but separate from them. (I wanted to be sure to remember to ask her if I could use it before I put it in my box.)

When she arrived home from school, she rushed into the kitchen, very indignant. "You didn't ask if you could use my picture. You shouldn't take my things without asking," she said. I soothed her bent feelings as best I could and explained that I had intended to ask. After she was reassured, I asked for permission to use her picture. She was happy then to let me borrow it.

I have always tried to make it a practice to ask permission to use the children's possessions. I want them to have respect for the rights and properties of others, and I know that example is one of the best teachers. This experience with my daughter really taught me how important it is to show respect to children regardless of their age.

We should also show our children respect by never reading their mail or private papers or journals. They should be able to have confidence that they can leave personal papers out in their rooms without fear of anyone invading their privacy. If they want to share things with us, that's great, and we encourage it.

However, we don't want them to ever feel that they have to hide things from prying eyes.

Another way we should show respect for our children's privacy is by knocking on their bedroom doors before we enter. A child's bedroom is his domain, and when we cross into it, we should have his permission. I know that some parents feel that it's their house and they can go anywhere they want to in it. Of course, logically this is true. But if we want to teach our children respect and courtesy, it is important for us to set the example for them. We are telling them by example that we love them and respect them enough to show them the courtesy of knocking on their door. All the children should also be taught to respect each other enough that they too will knock before entering.

Perhaps one of the most important things for us as parents to achieve is to always be friends with our children. Especially during their teenage years, we need to be their best friends. Being true friends means that we really consider their feelings—that we are truly empathetic. We should always try to understand them and treat them with consideration. We need to soothe their hurt feelings and listen patiently, without judging, to all their problems. Above all, we need to be there when they need us—not just physically, for they sometimes need all our mental attention focused on them also. We need to keep the doors of communication always open. There is no room for any kind of a generation gap in the type of friendship we need to have with our children.

We need to feel close to them, and they need to feel close to us—close enough to always be able to confide in us. And when they do confide in us, we must never, never break that confidence. If they should tell one of the parents something they don't wish the other parent to know, then we must respect their wishes. Otherwise,we run the risk of their never confiding in us.

We shouldn't ever embarrass our children in public. We shouldn't tell stories about them that would make them look less than the person they want to be. Their feelings must be considered in all circumstances. What may be very cute and funny to us may have a directly opposite effect on them. It is up to us to know them well enough to know what their reactions would be under such circumstances. We shouldn't scold them in front of their friends. We should show them the courtesy of waiting until their friends have left, or call them aside privately if it's something that can't wait.

Parents shouldn't use something their children have done or an experience of theirs as an example in teaching a class or giving a talk without first obtaining their permission. How would we feel if someone flaunted our mistakes in front of others or bragged about our accomplishments without first consulting us? Children have feelings, and perhaps there are some things they just don't want others to know about. I had occasion to sit in a mother education class in Relief Society in which a mother used an episode from her teenage daughter's life as an example. My heart ached for the girl as the mother related the incident. I couldn't help wondering how the girl would feel knowing many of the sisters in the ward knew what she had done. I also worried about the risk the mother was taking. Her daughter had several friends in the ward. I wondered how many of the mothers in the class would go home and carelessly tell their daughters what had happened with this girl. Would it eventually get back to her through her friends? Would it close a door between her and her mother? We must be so careful not to offend our children in this manner.

While our children were still quite young, we established a system of family government with them. When it was feasible, we let them help make decisions. For instance, when it came time to plan our vacations or holidays, we let them help decide what to do. When they were still quite small, we made the suggestions and then let them vote on what they wanted to do. We abided by the majority rule. When the children got older, we also let them make suggestions. This method of family government requires parents who are willing to give and not always have their way. Of course, we only let the children have a say on decisions we can logically turn over to a family vote. They don't totally run the family by any means, but the voting process gives them experience in decision making and lets them feel more a part of the family as they have a voice in family matters.

Christmas is a time when I have been outvoted many times. For years I wanted a flocked tree and the children wanted a big, old-fashioned one. We finally compromised when our house was large enough to accommodate two trees and all our feelings. Gerald has usually had to give in a little more in regard to vacations. Some of the things he wanted to see and do were things the children just weren't interested in. They preferred visiting relatives.

Because we have let the children have a say and have been

very open with them, we have been able to go a step further. After family home evening, Gerald goes around the group and asks if anyone has anything to say or any complaints to register. The children feel quite free to express themselves. We receive many helpful suggestions from this approach.

One suggestion I remember in particular was when our oldest daughter complained about our allowance system. She felt it needed revising since the children were older. We counseled about it and decided she was right, so we raised their allowances. Because they saw results from their suggestions, they were willing to make them. Children have a lot of good ideas that parents may fail to think of.

During the summer we let the children make suggestions for their weekend activities. When they were younger, they would often vote to go to the drive-in movie. This was really hard on Gerald, as he had such a total lack of interest in movies that he always slept through them. However, for a long time he went with us, slept there, and then drove us home. I finally decided that this was ridiculous. I suggested to the children that we leave Daddy at home to sleep, and I'd take them to the movie. They agreed. I was always a little nervous doing this, but we never ran into any problems. It's not always easy to take nine small children to a movie by yourself, but everyone cooperated. Doing things with the children that they want to do is truly a rewarding experience.

The whole secret, I guess, is doing things with them that we enjoy when they're small. Then when they're older, they vote to do those things. They feel good because they think we're doing what they want to do. We're reinforcing again by example that we really care for and love them.

In rearing children we need to forget ourselves and our age. Sometimes we need to let our hair down and be one with them. We need to go out and jump the rope with them. We need to draw a hopscotch and play with them. They really enjoy seeing us step on a line or stoop over to pick up our taw. We need to get down and play jacks with them, to teach them how. We need to go out and play leapfrog, and when we're out of breath they laugh at us. We need to play basketball with them and try guarding them when they're so quick and agile and we're tired. (It keeps us young!) We need to go swimming with them—to teach them how to swim and dive. Then we need to be patient as time after time they want us to watch them. We need to throw ball with them. We need to play No Bears Out Tonight and Red Rover, Red Rover. And when we're tired we take them for a nature walk and carry them piggy-back when they're tired. We need to revive all the old games we played as children and teach them to our children. We need to keep up with the times and learn the new ones they're playing.

When it's harvesting time, we need to take our children with us to pick fruit and vegetables. We need to let them learn as much as they can about food and how to handle it. And when we bring it home, we need to make canning and freezing a family project. The children will appreciate what they have much more if they've also shared in the preparation. Some of my fondest memories are of being up in a cherry tree with a child reminding him to spit out the stone as his little hands plop a big cherry into his mouth. Or watching all the children take part when we're making apricot nectar or preparing fruit to be dried or made into leather. How they love to go pick tomatoes, with a salt shaker tucked in their pockets.

One of the greatest ways you can be a friend to your children is to act their age *occasionally.* I emphasize occasionally because they still want us to be their parents. There needs to be a definite line drawn that creates the respect for an elder that a child should have, but this line needs to get thinned down once in a while. It doesn't hurt for us to let our hair down and join in the things they like to do.

When the children were small, Gerald always tried to take the week between Christmas and New Year's off so that we could spend the time together as a family. He spent much of the time during the day going sleigh-riding with the children; then at night we sat around and played games and ate popcorn. One particular year we all gathered in the family room in the basement around the big, white rock fireplace. The large pinon pine Christmas tree that the children loved and had decorated was there. The setting was beautiful and the snow and cold outside made the fire in the fireplace all the more cheerful. We spread out in a circle on the floor and began playing a game. As the evening wore on both children and parents became more enthusiastic and more loud. At ten o'clock Dad suggested it was time to quit, but we were far too excited to stop then. At eleven o'clock he suggested bed again, but no one was interested. By midnight he'd even quit suggesting. By one o'clock we had begun to run down slightly but not quite enough to quit. By two o'clock we were all ready to quit, but we had had so much fun together, no one wanted to leave. So we all gathered pillows and blankets and just camped out together on the family room floor. We did this for several nights, and it was really enjoyable for all of us. One night that floor just seemed too hard to sleep on, so my husband and I crept into the adjoining bedroom and slept on the twin beds in there. The children pounced on us early in the morning and accused us of cheating. We hurriedly explained that our bones were more brittle than theirs and needed a softer resting place.

That Christmas was such a special time. We were so close as a family. We all hated to see New Year's Day arrive and with it the return to realistic living, but life just had to go on. The experience had been great for all of us, though, not just for the fun and association, but as a learning experience. When we forget ourselves and join the children in what they want to do, we reap the greatest of rewards in close relationships.

Sunday night has also been a night when we have done things as a family. We always make a huge bowl of popcorn (or two or three). When we lived in Utah, in the winter we played games or put puzzles together. In the summer we went out on the grass to eat our popcorn and cool off. Soon the neighborhood children would join us. We had to start using the canning kettle to put the popcorn in so we'd have enough. The children would run happily across the grass and do somersaults down the hill on the side of our yard. My husband and I would wiggle our toes in the cool grass and watch contentedly as our children romped away. "Watch this, Mommie and Daddy," they'd call as they'd experiment on a cartwheel or a backbend. The little ones would roll down the hill, but would first call for our attention, as they wanted our recognition of their feats. How happy and content they all seemed to be—and it all took very little effort on our part.

When we moved to Arizona, traditions changed. Sunday night popcorn was still in, but the hot weather forced us indoors in the summer. The older children were excited to be living in the mission field and having contact with the full-time missionaries. Our oldest son always invited the elders over for popcorn. He attended early morning seminary and had a paper route to deliver before that, so he was often in bed when the elders arrived, but he still invited them. The children looked upon the elders as their older brothers, and each new set was accepted as family. They set a fine example for our children, and their presence made the whole idea of going on a mission much more real to our boys.

Sunday nights still mean popcorn and togetherness as a family, but as the children have gotten older, the evenings have changed. Often we just sit down together and have a good talk session while eating away at the popcorn. Sometimes we watch slides and reminisce about other times. Some of the children have meetings with the bishopric or firesides to attend, so on Sunday night there seems to be a lot of coming and going, but those who can still sit down with us. We have a bond of closeness that comes from many such evenings spent together in a harmonious and enjoyable way.

This is what life is all about. The joys and satisfaction that come from raising a family simply cannot be measured. Many a night we fall into bed thoroughly exhausted, but it's worth it. When they begin to leave home is really the only difficult time. We hope and pray as they go out into the world that we've done a thorough job—one that would be pleasing to their Heavenly Father. Has their training been sufficient? Has it been deep enough that they will carry with them the "mark of Mormonism" wherever they go? Only time will tell.

Index